ANYONE

NOT

EVERYONE

A PROVEN SYSTEM TO ESCAPE FOUNDER-LED SALES

— AGENCY EDITION —

COREY QUINN

Chapter Four originally appeared in the Forbes Agency Council column on Forbes.com.

Published by Reframe Press (reframepress.com)

Editing by Amanda Lewis Creative Inc. & Crissy Boylan
Book cover by Vanessa Mendozzi
Illustrations by Amy Williams Design

First edition 2024

Hardcover ISBN: 979-8-9896951-0-2
Softcover ISBN: 979-8-9896951-1-9
E-book ISBN: 979-8-9896951-2-6
Audiobook ISBN: 979-8-9896951-3-3

AnyoneNotEveryone.com

REFRAME
PRESS

Praise for *Anyone, Not Everyone*

"*Anyone, Not Everyone* gives you the ultimate road map to becoming the best loved agency for a focused vertical market. A must-read!"

—DR. BENJAMIN HARDY, author of *Be Your Future Self Now*

"*Anyone, Not Everyone* is an excellent guide for agency owners who want to escape founder-led sales with a targeted approach to sales and marketing for vertical markets. Corey's advice on effective positioning, messaging, and marketing campaigns is invaluable for any agency looking to specialize deeply and attract the best-fit clients."

—AARON ROSS, coauthor of *Predictable Revenue*
and *From Impossible to Inevitable*

"One of the secrets to great positioning is having compelling value aimed at a tightly defined target market. *Anyone, Not Everyone* is a must-read for agency owners looking to escape the trap of trying to serve a market that is fundamentally too broad."

—APRIL DUNFORD, positioning expert and author of *Obviously Awesome*

"Aim high, dig deep. Go big, think narrow. Corey unravels the specialization paradox, a lesson our agency learned the hard way, over way too many years. After reading *Anyone, Not Everyone*, you'll have the boldness to say *no thank you* to subpar clients, choosing conviction over constant yes-chasing."

—JOHN RUHLIN, founder and author of GIFT•OLOGY

"The days of the generalist marketing agency are over. If you aren't positioning yourself as a specialist and tightly defining your niche, you're doing business in hard mode. This book takes you through the process of deep specialization and will help you generate more revenue, attain greater freedom, and have more fun in the process."

—**ALLAN DIB**, author of *The 1-Page Marketing Plan*

"*Anyone, Not Everyone* isn't a book based on theory or opinion. The blueprint Corey lays out here helped us scale Scorpion 8x in five years. More importantly, these principles empowered us to better support thousands of business owners and their employees in our focus verticals. If you want to maximize the value of your product or service, choose the path of *Anyone, Not Everyone*, and let this book be your guide. Profitable revenue is sure to follow."

—**JAMIE ADAMS**, chief revenue officer at Scorpion

"When people ask me if I would have done anything differently, I say *no* except one thing: I would have chosen our niche from day one. We'd be 5x the size we are now. Corey has real-world insights because he's *actually done it*."

—**ALEX MEMBRILLO**, CEO of Cardinal Digital

"As an agency owner who struggled for years to extract myself from our sales process, I can tell you that Corey is addressing a critical (and all too common) problem in our industry. His vertical market approach can help you reclaim your time without sacrificing the sales growth that your agency needs to thrive."

—**CHRIS DREYER**, CEO of Rankings.io

"*Anyone, Not Everyone* is a goldmine of wisdom for agency owners. It's loaded with powerful, actionable advice and provides a clear blueprint for success through vertical market specialization. A must-read for those ready to take their agency to the next level."

—MIKE PEREZ, CEO of iLawyerMarketing

"This book absolutely hits the nail on the head. With this book, Corey is helping agencies around the world avoid the traps of running a generalist agency. *Anyone, Not Everyone* is the perfect tool that lays out actionable steps you can take to elevate your marketing agency, your relationships, and your life. Let's go!"

—LUKE EGGEBRAATEN, founder of Phaser Marketing and author of *The Digital Dirt World*

"This is one of the most important books I have read in a long time and is a must-read for all agency owners regardless of size. In an incredibly crowded agency world, verticalization is a necessary step to scale, and Corey Quinn's five step process provides the detailed road map on how to do it. I will absolutely be recommending this book to all of my clients."

—JON MORRIS, CEO of EngineBI and founder of Rise Interactive

"As someone who audits agency profitability for a living, I can tell you specialization is the common thread between all the top-performing firms. If you only read one book on how to accomplish meaningful specialization that dramatically improves your agency's performance, this should be that book."

—MARCEL PETITPAS, CEO and cofounder of Parakeeto Inc.

"Corey's stellar track record has established him as an authority in helping agencies unlock their growth. Had his book and guidance been available during our Fanscape growth journey, it would have been a game-changer. If you're looking for actionable insights and a strategic edge in your agency's growth, do yourself a favor and get this book."

—**TERRY DRY**, cofounder of Fanscape (sold to Omnicom)

"As someone who has personally worked with over 300 agencies, I can confidently say that agencies who struggle to specialize will struggle to succeed. We've heard 'the riches are in the niches,' but there hasn't been a proven agency framework on *how* to actually carve out that niche—until now. This book should not just be read; it should be studied. Corey is a true practitioner who has actually put this guide to work in the trenches throughout his career and is kind enough to now share it with the rest of us."

—**JOEY GILKEY**, CEO of Apex Revenue

"Corey captures the essence of what has made great companies successful for years: *focus*, concentration on the critical few and not on the trivial many. Creating customers is different than making money. He highlights *the* path to growth for agency businesses: the founder has to get out of the way if the business is to thrive. This is a must-read if you want your agency to be more than a mom-and-pop shop. Kudos, Corey!"

—**RORY J. CLARK**, creator of the Focus Selling Customer Development System, gofocusselling.com

"Sure, you know you should 'niche down' to get your agency to the next level, but how do you actually do it? In *Anyone, Not Everyone*, Corey provides a proven step-by-step process for beating the competition through deep specialization. This isn't just theory; it's the road map he used to grow recurring revenue at Scorpion from $20 million to $150 million in under seven years. Solid gold!"

—**JONATHAN STARK**, advisor to professional services firms

"*Anyone, Not Everyone* offers digital marketing agencies a timely and practical guide for breaking through the noise by specializing within a niche vertical market. With today's ultra-competitive landscape, generalist agencies spread themselves thin and rely on discounting, resulting in bland messaging that blends into the clutter. Corey Quinn makes the case that intentional specialization—thoroughly understanding a niche audience to provide tailored solutions—is the path to sustainable growth and an unassailable competitive advantage. This book delivers an actionable playbook for agencies to transform themselves, from choosing a vertical market to crafting specialized campaigns, guiding readers to establish their agency as an indispensable pillar within a chosen community.

If I had used this approach with the website development agency I owned and operated for six years, there is *no way* I wouldn't have increased my growth multiple times over. Corey has provided a guide that, if followed, could change the entire trajectory of your business. Do yourself a favor and pay attention!"

—**MARK DE GRASSE**, president of Digital Marketer

Download the Audiobook Free!

READ THIS FIRST

To say thanks for purchasing my book, I'd like to give you the audiobook version 100% FREE!

I know this book can and will transform your business ... and you're more likely to finish it if you have the audiobook.

Plus, I am the narrator, so it'll be like having a personal chat.

AnyoneNotEveryone.com/audio

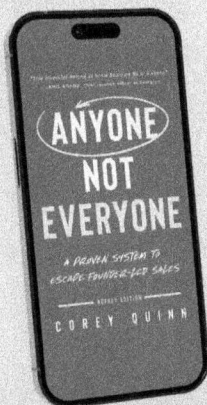

ANYONE
NOT
EVERYONE

A PROVEN SYSTEM TO
ESCAPE FOUNDER-LED SALES

COREY QUINN

Contents

To entrepreneurs everywhere who are working as hard on improving themselves as they are on improving their business.

ADDITIONAL RESOURCES FOR YOU

Follow this link directly to the book's resource page,
where you'll find videos and a companion workbook.

AnyoneNotEveryone.com

"The number
one question in
a consumer's
mind today is
'Who can I trust?'"

JOE POLISH

Introduction

magine sending $1 million worth of gourmet chocolate chip cookies to thousands of unsuspecting potential clients you've never before contacted.

That sounds like a great way to waste $1 million, right? Wrong.

In fact, this tactic helped put the last agency I worked for on its way to growing revenue from $20 million to $150 million in just over six years.

And it has worked for my clients as well.

Don't get me wrong. Blindly sending gourmet cookies to potential clients is not the surefire solution to your growth challenges.

Sending gourmet cookies is a small part of a larger, completely innovative sales and marketing methodology I call **Deep Specialization**. It's the product of my 15 years of experience in agency sales and marketing, blended with effective strategies from successful vertical agencies and from across the disciplines of product marketing, sales, positioning, category design, and messaging.

This book will walk you through the principles, strategies, and tactics of Deep Specialization so you can apply it directly to your agency.

HERE'S THE BACKSTORY

In 2015, after selling digital agency services for eight years, I had come to believe that founder-led sales was just how the agency business worked. The agency founder would source the deals, and the sales rep would close them.

One founder I worked for was a Harvard Business School graduate. His professional network provided an abundant source of warm leads from brand-name CEOs and CMOs. Another founder was the former CEO of Myspace (yes, that Myspace). He, too, had a fantastic network of CEOs and business leaders. He was a brilliant networker, creating new opportunities for the agency with seeming ease.

Sure, over the years, we tried supplementing what the founder brought into the agency. We built a sales team, hired third-party cold callers, and created thought-leadership content pieces.

Some approaches worked okay. Most didn't work at all.

We always defaulted to what worked best: deals the founder brought in.

WHAT CHANGED?

When I arrived at an agency called Scorpion in 2015 as their new chief marketing officer, it was my responsibility to grow revenue for the already successful $20 million agency.

But this agency was different. It had already built a name for itself within the legal industry. Scorpion targeted personal injury attorneys. And generating new business was not dependent on the founder's network.

Instead, attorneys would Google their local competitors using terms such as "attorney in my area," find a Scorpion client website, and see a Scorpion logo and link to our website at the bottom.

These links drove warm inbound leads to our sales team that often resulted in a one-call close, followed by a strike of the massive metallic gong on the sales floor and high fives all around by the sales team.

GONNNNGGG!

These attorneys had no idea who Scorpion's founder was, nor did they care. It was like a popular restaurant where the delicious food was the main attraction, not the celebrity chef. What they cared about was finding a reliable, proven partner with expertise in attorney marketing that they could trust to help them get more clients from internet traffic.

I quickly realized that attorneys preferred partnering with a vertical specialist over generalists. They would say yes faster to a company that knew their business well than to a generalist agency where they were one among many types of clients. And they would happily pay a premium.

A vertical specialist can gain clients and scale the business without leaning on the founder's personal network.

Attorneys were not only choosing to work with an attorney marketing specialist agency, but they also stayed over the long run. Scorpion had a 93% retention rate, whereas most competitors only retained 70%.

Scorpion's legal vertical specialization not only helped them become one of the most well-known and respected agencies with attorneys, but it also laid the groundwork for launching three additional vertical markets—home services, franchise, and medical—which propelled the agency to $150 million in under seven years.

WHAT IS A VERTICAL MARKET?

Before we go too far down the road, let's define a vertical market.

A vertical is a market where vendors, such as agencies, offer services specific to an industry, trade, profession, or other group of customers with specialized needs. It's distinct from a horizontal market, where vendors offer a broad range of goods and services to a large group of customers with a wide range of needs.

Think of it this way:

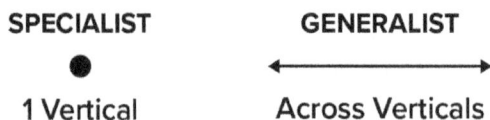

SPECIALIST	GENERALIST
●	←————————→
1 Vertical	Across Verticals

In a vertical market approach, you tailor your services to satisfy the needs of a particular industry segment (a "vertical"). Examples of vertical markets include:

- **Healthcare:** Medical practices, hospitals, and pharmaceutical companies.
- **Home Services:** Plumbers, HVAC technicians, roofers, and electricians.
- **Real Estate:** Property managers, real estate brokers, leasing agents, and property appraisers.
- **Hospitality and Tourism:** Hotels, resorts, travel agencies, tour operators, and other services catering to travelers.

WHAT IS DEEP SPECIALIZATION?

Deep Specialization is the disciplined practice of intentionally specializing your agency for businesses within a specific vertical market in order to gain a distinctive advantage. It requires focus, empathy, and strategy. Here's a breakdown:

Focus: Commit to one vertical so you can say no to many others.

Empathy: Care for the vertical and the people in it.

Strategy: Design a massive action plan to create a durable competitive advantage.

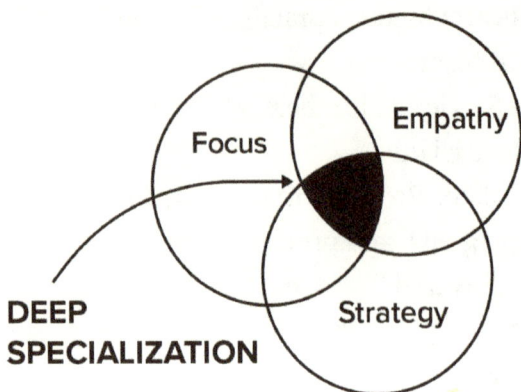

Focus · Empathy · Strategy · **DEEP SPECIALIZATION**

DEEP SPECIALIZATION AT WORK

Here are two examples of how shifting from a generalized to a specialized approach can transform your agency.

Sarah Durham is the founder and former CEO of a well-respected communications firm for nonprofits called Big Duck (which she sold to her employees in 2021). She started her firm in 1994 as a generalist marketing agency, and six years in, after serving all kinds of clients across all kinds of industries, she felt like the business was running her instead of her running the business.

She decided to specialize on the nonprofit sector—a vertical market. This decision was the catalyst for tremendous growth for her and her company, lasting decades. As Sarah told me in a recent interview, "Every successful decision ... probably cascaded out of that moment of choosing to specialize."[1]

Alex Membrillo is the founder and CEO of a healthcare marketing agency called Cardinal Digital Marketing, which focuses on multi-location medical practices. He started his agency as a generalist serving everyone from an ice cream van operator to attorneys to roofers. After several years, his agency was sputtering with slow sales and poor retention. It was at that point he became determined to choose a single vertical. He chose medical practices and has since built his agency to eight figures.[2]

Listen to more stories on my show, *The Deep Specialization Podcast* (coreyquinn.com/dsp). I interview dozens of agency owners who started as generalists and found remarkable success as vertical market specialists.

WHO SHOULD READ THIS BOOK?

This book is for ambitious agency founders and their teams who are:

- Ready to escape founder-led sales and remove the barriers holding them back from building a scaled-up agency to seven, eight, or nine figures.
- Overcommitted, busy, and tired of delivering work that is "good enough," secretly knowing it could be better.
- Running an undifferentiated, commoditized, jack-of-all-trades agency for clients of all shapes and sizes.
- Already vertically focused but aren't experiencing the growth they want.

WHAT TO EXPECT

In this book, I'll teach you Deep Specialization, showing you the path from generalist to vertical market specialist.

In **Part One**, I'll lay out the argument for becoming a vertical market specialist and why it's a great way to scale an agency.

In **Part Two**, I'll walk you through the five steps to Deep Specialization so you can transform your agency into a vertical market specialist.

DEEP SPECIALIZATION

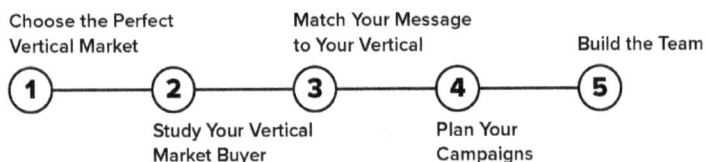

Choose the Perfect
Vertical Market

Match Your Message
to Your Vertical

Build the Team

(1) —— **(2)** —— **(3)** —— **(4)** —— **(5)**

Study Your Vertical
Market Buyer

Plan Your
Campaigns

- Step 1: I'll show you how to quickly choose your best-fit vertical.
- Step 2: I'll teach you how to uncover the unique needs, desires, and fears of your vertical market's buyers.
- Step 3: I'll show you how to match your message to your buyer, differentiate your agency, and create a point of view that attracts best-fit clients.
- Step 4: I'll reveal the best vertical-specific sales and marketing strategies to fill your pipeline and grow your agency.

- Step 5: I'll share what team resources you'll need and which roles you should hire in-house or outsource, as well as my final thoughts on ensuring your success with Deep Specialization.

I have intentionally kept the content light on theory: by focusing on tactical execution, this book will help you implement Deep Specialization directly to your agency. I wrote it as a guide for you, the ambitious founder, marketer, and entrepreneur. My goal is to help you adopt the winning principles, strategies, and tactics that propelled hundreds of agencies from a struggling market generalist to a successful vertical specialist.

Are you ready to leave behind being overstretched and providing results that are "good enough" and transform into a business owner whose lucrative agency has earned an outstanding reputation for providing its clients exceptional results?

Let's do this!

Part One

Specializing in a Vertical Market Is the Key to Growth

Chapter 1

Anyone, Not Everyone

"The difference between successful people
and really successful people is that really
successful people say no to almost everything."

WARREN BUFFETT, businessman, investor, and philanthropist[3]

S aying yes to too many different types of clients
leads to long hours, stressful multitasking, and
anxiety-producing context switching. You're con-
stantly putting out client fires and jumping from one
urgent task to the next. Worse, you're not making real
progress towards your growth goals.

Now imagine a different situation: your agency is
filled with one type of client—your best-fit clients.

Your best-fit clients are uniquely suited for your agency,
and you are uniquely suited for them. They're a subset of
the clients you already have. They get outstanding results

with you, and they generate great revenue for you. They stay with you the longest and will happily sign long-term contracts. They have short sales cycles and the highest levels of satisfaction. They evangelize your agency to their friends and colleagues without being asked to.

Your sales team is most confident selling to them. Your client success team enjoys working with them the most. You like them too: they don't complain, they give kudos, and they feel like a partner, not a customer.

So, if you could fill your business with these types of clients, would you?

Of course you would, as would any agency founder who values their time, profit, and freedom.

The good news? There are enough of them in the market to justify focusing only on them.

The better news? Doing so is not only possible but easy to achieve with the *right strategy*.

CUT THROUGH THE NOISE

You may not want to hear this, but ambitious entrepreneurs are launching nimble yet impressive enterprises designed to steal your current and future clients.

They're eagerly cold-calling, emailing, and publishing thought leadership content. They're deploying sophisticated pay-per-click (PPC), TikTok, and LinkedIn strategies. They're using generative AI to create lead magnets, building Facebook communities, launching podcasts that target your ideal clients, and more.

Complicating this, your current and future clients are vulnerable to making poor buying decisions that not only hurt their own businesses but yours. They don't notice the difference between your reliable solution to their problem and the flimsy solution offered by a fly-by-night upstart.

You're left grasping for a way to cut through the chaos so you can grow a profitable and sustainable agency business.

The answer is to become a vertical specialist.

> Specializing in a vertical market is the shortest path to gaining visibility and trust for your business in today's ultra-competitive world.

HOW TO SPECIALIZE YOUR AGENCY

There are two ways to specialize your agency business.

Who You Serve

Do you serve businesses of all shapes and sizes? Do you specialize in serving a super narrow vertical market? Or something in between?

For example, a digital agency serving doctors is more specialized than an agency serving all types of service businesses. However, an agency exclusively serving cosmetic surgeons would be even more specialized than one serving any kind of doctor.

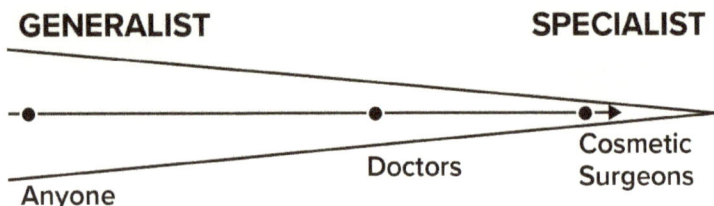

GENERALIST   **SPECIALIST**

Anyone   Doctors   Cosmetic Surgeons

What You Do

Do you provide a broad suite of services? Do you specialize in providing just one service? Or something in between?

For example, a digital agency that does content marketing is more specialized than an agency doing all things digital. However, an agency that exclusively does TikTok videos would be even more specialized.

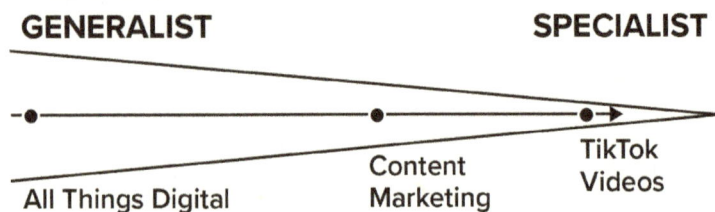

GENERALIST   **SPECIALIST**

All Things Digital   Content Marketing   TikTok Videos

Deep Specialization Pro Tip: Blend a specialization in both *who you serve* and *what you do* to greatly differentiate your agency's brand. For example, "We specialize in making TikTok videos for cosmetic surgeons."

THE CHALLENGES OF BEING A GENERALIST

Does this sound familiar?

Your agency is really good at search engine optimization and PPC (or your particular service or expertise). You're a member of YPO[4] and Vistage,[5] and by networking in these groups, you've attracted a lot of new business.

A few years in, you've built up a decent portfolio of agency clients, including a multi-location moving company, a cosmetology school, a credit union, an office furniture supply company, an industrial manufacturer, a wealth management firm, a national CPA firm, a storage rental company, a cooking supplies company, a hotel, and a hospital.[6] All told, you have clients across 11 very different vertical markets.

Sure, the revenue is good, but you and your team secretly dread bringing on each new client, which represents yet another new industry that you don't know much about. Each new client means you must learn another industry.

Each new client means more multitasking and context shifting for your team. Each new client requires more meetings and synchronous communication. Each new client is a tax on your finite resources.

The cumulative result is work that is good enough but barely satisfying to you or the client. It's no wonder your clients are leaving you for agencies that specialize in their vertical market.

Making matters worse, generating new sales for the agency is inextricably tied to you as the founder. If you're not sourcing new deals and closing them, the agency doesn't grow. Sure, you want to scale up your sales, but nothing seems to work. Plus, your buyer sees your service as an interchangeable commodity so there's ever increasing pressure to discount.

You apply a "peanut butter" approach to marketing your agency. Your messaging is bland and easy to ignore. You rely on the same tired claims every other agency uses: "We're an extension of your team" and "We care about your success."

Compounding all this: you have no time to innovate. Your reactive approach to applying new and disruptive technologies like generative AI leaves you susceptible to getting priced out of the market.

In fact, nothing about your agency is particularly remarkable.

What Got You Here Won't Get You There

Agency owners eventually realize that saying yes to any client who wants to work with them is the strategy that got them in the game, but now it's the very thing that's holding them back.

Luke Eggebraaten, founder of Phaser Marketing, a fast-growing seven-figure agency targeting construction companies, told me about this moment for him:

> What we really changed is we started turning away people that wanted to work with us. People that had checks in hand ready to pay us. That was hard. But I'm so glad we stuck through with it.
>
> And we just said, "Nope, we do digital marketing for construction companies. I'm sorry."
>
> And they're like, "Well, yeah, but I have $5,000 for you."
>
> [And we said] "I will refer you to somebody that can help."
>
> And people all of a sudden started respecting that.[7]

THERE IS A DIFFERENT WAY

But why specialize in a vertical market? Isn't it risky to put all your eggs in one basket?

Specializing isn't only about limiting scope or streamlining operations: it's about unlocking the true potential of your agency by becoming the master of one domain.

That's what Deep Specialization is all about.

In the next chapter, we'll uncover the many benefits of vertical market specialization and delve into how this targeted approach isn't just a strategy—it's the future of sustainable and exponential growth for your agency.

Dive in, and let's redefine success.

CHAPTER TAKEAWAYS

- Be selective with your clients for better outcomes for your agency.
- Align your agency's strengths and offerings with the right vertical market.
- In the modern ultra-competitive landscape, you're vying for the same clients as many other businesses.
- Stand out by being different.

Chapter 2

Six Reasons to Become a Vertical Market Specialist

"In a busy marketplace, not standing out is the same as being invisible."

SETH GODIN, author of *Purple Cow*[8]

After five years working with anyone who would hire them, Joe Sullivan and his partner at marketing agency Gorilla 76 decided to be honest with themselves. They explored what they liked doing, what they were good at doing, and where they were profitable. This led them to decide to specialize in industrial manufacturing clients. In his interview with me, he shared:

"I remember it being a little bit scary when we changed whatever it said on our homepage at the time, probably some ridiculous statement about how we do everything for everybody. That was a big shift."

The result?

Today, they run a multimillion-dollar specialist marketing agency that deeply understands their client base, is differentiated in the market, and laser-focused on providing outsized results for their clients in the industrial manufacturing vertical. In other words, they're Deep Specialists.

From Joe's perspective, "The benefits [of specializing] far outweigh the risks and challenges."[9]

Let's talk about the benefits of becoming a vertical market specialist.

BENEFIT 1: SIMPLIFIES SALES AND MARKETING

It's like having a map when traveling through unfamiliar territory. By focusing on a single vertical market, you immediately know where to go. You know which:

- Buyers to target
- Conversion copy to write
- Lists to build
- Content to create
- PPC keywords to buy
- SEO keywords to rank for
- Conferences to speak at
- Case studies to produce
- Data points to create

- Associations to get involved with
- Competitors to research
- Podcasts to start
- Podcasts to be a guest on
- ... and so much more

This specificity and clarity saves you time and makes your sales and marketing infinitely more impactful.

BENEFIT 2: IMPROVES SALES CONFIDENCE

Salespeople crush quotas in environments where they have momentum and confidence. By selling into a single market, they'll become familiar with the vertical buyer's business, including their unique pains and problems.

Your salespeople will become more knowledgeable about the business than your buyer when it comes to marketing (or your service area of focus), allowing them to teach and guide the buyer during the sales process. This elevates your sales conversations out of marketing tactics and into business strategy, resulting in more value for your prospect and distinguishing your agency from competitors.

They'll also learn the buyer's insider language, industry trends, and major players.

The result is more trust and familiarity, which leads to more sales.

"Your salespeople get more confident [by specializing on a vertical]. Some of our HVAC salespeople could probably walk into an HVAC company today and actually be pretty good general managers or operational managers. The result? They're probably gonna sell more things."

JAMIE ADAMS, chief revenue officer at Scorpion[10]

BENEFIT 3: REMOVES FRICTION FROM THE BUYING PROCESS

Have you ever lived in San Francisco?

If so, chances are you don't say "San Fran." Maybe you say "SF" or "the city," but never, ever "San Fran." Merely saying "San Fran" in the greater Bay Area immediately exposes someone as an outsider.

You wouldn't know this unless you were an insider.

People who live in a city (like San Francisco), work in a trade (like plumbers), or are part of an industry (like higher education) use an insider language based on shared experiences, skills, or values. You can call it jargon, lingo, or slang, but using it in a group signals you belong.

Naturally, those outside the group don't know the lingo, and if they use a word or term that exposes them as an outsider, they are held at arm's length.

Here's an example: Do you know what an FDD is? How about an NAF? Or an LMP?[11] Chances are, if you're not from the franchise industry, you'll have no idea. But people in the franchise industry use these terms every day. If you were trying to sell your agency services to a franchise brand and they happened to ask you something like, "Does this get funded by the NAF?" your response would immediately reveal whether you are an insider or an outsider.

While learning your buyer's lingo isn't necessarily a groundbreaking idea, the reason it's important is buyers in a vertical market care greatly about whether you can solve their *specific* problem, not a *generic* version of their problem. One of the ways you communicate that you're capable of solving their specific problem is by knowing their insider language.

Your buyers care a lot about working with people who truly understand them. They want to work with insiders. Knowing you're an insider removes some of the friction in the buying process.

Chris Yano, founder of RYNO Strategic Solutions, an eight-figure digital marketing agency specializing in HVAC companies, told me, "Being an expert in their field comforts your buyers because they know you know their business."[12]

Being an insider is a key differentiator and competitive advantage for your agency.

How Do You Learn the Insider Language of Your Vertical Buyer?

Spend lots of time with your vertical buyer, solve their problems, and truly care about them and their success.

Meet with them regularly, join their associations and social media groups, and read their industry publications. Over time, you'll pick up on patterns of insider words and phrases, and you'll begin to understand what they mean within the greater context of their world.

Want a shortcut? Attend a conference.

Allan Dib, author of *The 1-Page Marketing Plan*, explains: "I attended a conference for the pharmacy industry and in half a day of hanging out with these people, I knew more about the industry, their pain points, what they're suffering with, what their hopes, what their dreams, what their desires are than if I spent six months online trying to figure it out. Now I can enter that conversation going on in their mind."[13]

Take note of their key phrases and adopt them in your communication (for example, your website, collateral, marketing, sales) to signal that you're a part of the tribe.

Your generalist competitors might claim to be specialists (and fake it), or they won't go to this level of detail in their language, much less in their service offering.

"You may use their insider words, but they're still gonna sniff you out. You should be smart enough to say no and go, 'We don't know that; we're gonna get killed in this pitch.' Or worst case, we're gonna get hired and then we're gonna suck. So why would you do that?"

TERRY DRY, cofounder of Fanscape (sold to Omnicom)[14]

Deep Specialization Pro Tip: Join active social media groups in your vertical market and observe the ongoing conversations to accelerate your knowledge of insider language.

BENEFIT 4: MAKES YOU EXTRAORDINARY

As Dan Sullivan and Dr. Benjamin Hardy write in their book *10x Is Easier Than 2x*, "Whatever you focus on, you develop a finer, more nuanced, and more specific understanding of." [15]

When you focus your time and energy on serving

clients in your chosen vertical market over an extended period, you notice patterns that generalists miss.

Noticing and acting on these subtle patterns improves your marketing, sales, and the value of the service you provide. This client intimacy leads to your agency exceeding your client's expectations, and when you do that repeatedly over time, you build loyalty and generate word-of-mouth recommendations.

Here's an example: Imagine for a moment that you own a lead gen marketing agency that exclusively works with plumbers. Not attorneys and plumbers, not roofers and plumbers, not HVAC and plumbers. Just plumbers.

Day in and day out, the only thing you and your team do is help plumbers find leads generated from the internet. You're a plumbing vertical market specialist.

After months of serving your plumber clients every single day, you learn that out of the 25 different types of plumbing jobs your clients can do for a residential client—everything from clogged drains to pipe leaks to water heater replacement—what they really want are repiping jobs.

A repiping job means a plumber is called in to install a whole new system of hot and cold water lines across an entire house. Plumbers love these jobs because they're multi-day, high-margin jobs that don't require messing with a stinky sewer line.

Armed with this knowledge, you build a marketing system that over time consistently and reliably finds repiping jobs for your plumber clients. It's not perfect at first, but with effort, you become the best in the country.

In other words, through specialization, you're able to provide significantly greater value to your plumber clients than your generalist competitors ever could. Specializing allows you to become an expert in solving hard, expensive problems for a specific audience. When you become a specialist, you're rare and valuable, so there's no limit to the demand for your services.

If you're concerned that narrowly targeting a vertical such as plumbers is thinking too small, you may want to think again.

There are 156,986 plumbing businesses in the U.S. today.[16] Assuming you had just 3% of the plumber market, you'd have 4,709 plumbers as clients. If your average annual revenue per client is $10,000, your plumbing-only lead gen company would be doing $47,090,000 annually. Not bad!

Deep Specialization Pro Tip: Anyone perceived as an industry generalist is usually the lowest paid.

BENEFIT 5: SCALES THROUGH SYSTEMS

When you market to, sell, and service a specific client in your vertical market over and over, certain aspects of your business will become repetitive ... and this is a good thing.

You'll begin to recognize patterns in how and why they buy, what offers they respond to, what inside language they use, which conferences they attend, which podcasts they listen to, and so on. You'll also notice emerging patterns as you serve them as clients. For example, you'll see how they like to be onboarded. Do they like a hands-on approach? Or would they prefer watching onboarding videos? How often do they want to be contacted? And so on.

These patterns allow you to refine and improve the quality and impact of your sales, marketing, and client service. They also pave the way for you to build systems to scale up your business.

Documented processes ensure the most important things get done the right way, every time, by everyone. I recommend creating an easily shared and globally accessible document for each business process (e.g., in Google Docs or another tool of your choice). As you and your team use those documented processes, look for manual, repeatable actions that don't require human effort. It could be a copy and paste here, an email notification there, an update to a project plan everywhere. And so on.

For these actions that don't require human interaction, you can use software. For example, instead of asking your clients to send an email every time they want to make a change to their website, have them fill out a simple form that collects everything your designers need. This way, your designers can quickly fulfill the request asynchronously and without relying on intermediaries like project managers or client success teams.

Using software to automate these tasks frees up your human capital (i.e., you and your team) to work on higher-value activities that can't or shouldn't be automated, such as connecting with clients.

Systems remove everyday human error that can negatively impact your client's experience and your business's reputation. Systems also reduce the need for synchronous communication, instead allowing your team to work more independently.

As you grow, your systems will improve the consistency of the value you create. Providing a high-value service consistently over time results in more new clients.

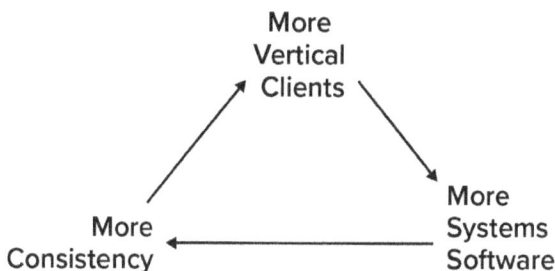

More
Vertical
Clients

More
Consistency

More
Systems
Software

Deep Specialization Pro Tip: Empower your team to own the creation and upkeep of process documentation to ensure that your system is accurate, used, and effective.

BENEFIT 6: ACCELERATES WORD OF MOUTH

Business owners and professionals prefer to socialize with others in their vertical. My wife, for example, is a psychiatrist and a mom. Guess how she likes to relax? Connecting and chatting in the Physician Mom group on Facebook. As of this writing, the Physician Mom group on Facebook has 80,700 members and about 200 posts every day.

Here's another example. There are approximately 17,000 new-car dealerships in the U.S. While not every dealership owner knows every other owner personally, they're all within one degree of separation. This means the owner of the BMW dealership in Santa Monica, California, is one phone call away from the owner of the Porsche dealership in Portland, Oregon.

This networked characteristic within a vertical is further amplified at natural gathering spots, like trade conferences, member associations, and online communities.

For example, dentists have dozens of conferences every year, including the Greater New York Dental Meeting, which 9,692 dentists attended in 2022. The American Dental Association has more than 161,000 members, and the Dentists in Facebook group alone has 41,400 members.

In addition to asking colleagues for referrals, people in a vertical market want to know *how* the top-performing business owners have an edge, especially when what they're doing is new and driving unusually good results. It's human nature to talk. And the innate network effect that exists within a vertical is put on steroids at conferences and events.

When you provide outsized results for your clients, your reputation within that vertical will grow, and word about you will naturally spread. Call it going viral or word of mouth, it is the holy grail of marketing because it means your current happy clients are spreading your agency's brand for free.

Positive word of mouth and referrals compound over time within a vertical market, allowing you to rely less on expensive paid media and advertising in the long run.

"From an agency perspective, once you hit the hundred client threshold, that's where it starts to really take off. Your clients are gonna refer you, the relationships you've made with everyone in this industry ... are gonna refer you."

RYAN GOLGOSKY, founder of 180 Sites[17]

Deep Specialization Pro Tip: As you enter your vertical's preexisting networks, find ways to create value by answering questions and generally being helpful.

So, how do you choose your vertical market? In the next chapters, I'll teach you how to identify the deep specialization that's perfect for your agency.

CHAPTER TAKEAWAYS

When you adopt a vertical market approach:

- Sales and marketing become simpler, more efficient, and effective.
- Your sales team builds confidence, momentum, and impact.
- Being an insider removes friction from the buying process.
- You exceed your client's expectations with deep, targeted insights.
- You turn repetitive patterns into effective systems for scale.
- You deliver superior service, retain more clients, and build word of mouth.

Part Two

Five Steps to Deep Specialization

DEEP SPECIALIZATION

Choose the Perfect
Vertical Market

Match Your Message
to Your Vertical

Build the Team

(1)———(2)———(3)———(4)———(5)

Study Your Vertical
Market Buyer

Plan Your
Campaigns

Step 1

Choose the Perfect Vertical Market

Chapter 3
Lay the Groundwork

M any founders I speak with think they already know which vertical market they should focus on, and you may feel the same way. Sure, you know your business and client base better than anyone else ... and your instincts are probably right.

However, I'll offer you the same advice I give my clients: even though you already know which vertical market to focus on, investing the time to validate your choice is worth the effort.

Why? Choosing a vertical market that *isn't* right for you and your business is a distraction at best, and a waste of years of your life (and potential revenue) at worst.

Invest a few hours and do this process the right way,

the first time. You'll avoid the heartbreak of realizing somewhere down the road that your hastily chosen vertical market isn't a long-term fit.

🕐 Assuming you have easy access to your client data, you're looking at:

- Under an hour to complete the exercises in Chapter 5
- An hour or two of basic market research

SHOULD MY VERTICAL COME FROM MY CURRENT CLIENT LIST?

The history you have with your current and past clients is the best and most reliable tool for choosing the right vertical market for your business. I'll walk you through how to use your client data to choose your vertical market in Chapter 5.

If you don't have client data or a track record, it's necessary to make educated guesses, especially when you're venturing into a new vertical or starting a new business. These guesses are not necessarily about market details of the vertical like its size, industry growth, or economic trends, as such information is usually easy to get.

To inform your decision, look for agencies and service-based businesses—such as accounting or law firms and consultants—that are already catering to the vertical market you're interested in. If you discover others have successfully engaged with this market, it's a good sign that it's a promising opportunity for you too.

WHEN SHOULD I CHOOSE A VERTICAL MARKET?

Usually, an agency evolves from being generalist to specialist over time. In the early phases, it's wise not to be overly selective about the clients you serve, as this period is crucial for understanding the wider market and trying to keep the lights on. Avoid rushing into specialization.

Paul Graham, founder of Y Combinator, advises early stage startups to **"do things that don't scale."**[19] Starting out by helping a lot of different businesses can be beneficial as it provides a clearer insight into the market dynamics.

The goal is to identify a sweet spot where there is alignment between your inherent strengths, your market demand, and who you're best at serving. This alignment will guide you in choosing the right vertical market for your agency.

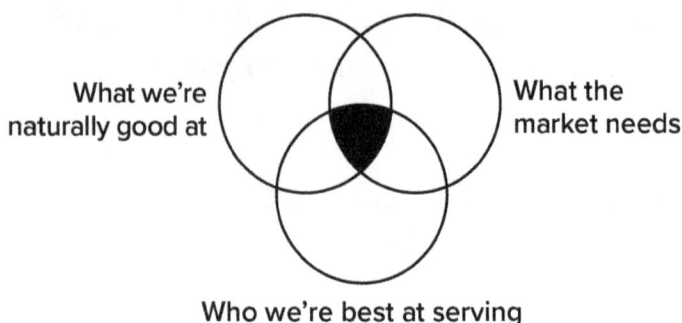

What we're naturally good at

What the market needs

Who we're best at serving

This learning process includes saying yes to businesses that may not initially seem like a perfect fit. What was once a tentative yes could turn out to be your best-fit client profile down the road, but you won't know unless you say yes.

Deep Specialization Pro Tip: Say yes often in the early days of your agency to gain a greater awareness of your strengths. By saying yes more often at the start, you can say no more often once you specialize.

WHAT MAKES A GOOD VERTICAL?

As you begin to work through the steps of selecting a vertical market using client data (discussed in Chapter 5), it's crucial to understand the characteristics of preferable and less preferable verticals. Here's a comparison to guide you.

Vertical Dynamics

	Preferable	Less Preferable
Revenue	The average annual revenue for businesses in the vertical is over $1,000,000.	The average annual business revenue is below $1,000,000.
Community	The vertical has a close-knit community, like music labels, franchises, or auto dealers.	The vertical is characterized by a loose or disconnected community (e.g., local neighborhoods).
Industry Language	Extensive use of jargon, acronyms, and insider sayings.	Little use of insider language or jargon.
Market Growth	The industry is on the rise (e.g., artificial intelligence, electric vehicles).	The industry is shrinking or in decline (e.g., newspapers, gas-powered vehicles).
Professional Requirements	Operating in this field requires certifications, licenses, or degrees (e.g., doctors, CPAs, attorneys).	No need for certifications, licenses, or degrees to operate a business.
Associations and Conferences	This vertical has at least two dedicated associations and conferences.	The vertical has none or only one dedicated association or conference.
Personal or Familial Connection	You have a personal or family connection to the industry (e.g., plumbing if your parents owned a plumbing company).	The thought of spending vast amounts of time with individuals in this vertical repels you.

	Preferable	Less Preferable
Professional Connection	You have prior experience or connections in the industry.	You have no prior knowledge or experience in the industry.
Existing Recognition	Your agency already has a presence or recognition within the vertical.	You and your business are not known within the vertical.

Remember, the goal is to find the right intersection between your strengths, market needs, and the clients you serve best. It's not just about finding a market but ensuring that it aligns with your expertise and passion.

In the next chapter, we'll cover the critical importance of empathy in creating success with Deep Specialization.

CHAPTER TAKEAWAYS

- Even if you think you know the right vertical market, take the time to validate it. Misjudging can result in a significant loss of time and effort.
- Your history with current and past clients can guide you in choosing the right vertical market.
- It's often beneficial to begin as a generalist, gather information, and then specialize based on your insights.
- Make sure you understand the characteristics of a good vertical—and what to avoid.

Chapter 4
Give a Damn

"The successful agencies of the future will be those that integrate technological excellence with profoundly human qualities: combining efficacy with empathy."

JIM CARROLL, former chairman of Bartle Bogle Hegarty[20]

The essence of Deep Specialization mirrors that of effective parenting—the ability to genuinely care. This caring, or empathy, is about valuing your clients and being invested in pushing both their business and their industry forward. Simply put: you need to give a damn.

On your agency journey, a significant amount of your time will be spent engaging with clients—be it in one-on-one meetings, group discussions, or networking at industry events. Unlike a switch, empathy cannot be turned on when convenient, nor can its importance be underestimated.

Dedicating your efforts to serve a vertical market is like pacing yourself in a marathon over terrain that oscillates between peaks and valleys. There will be periods when your vertical's industry is expanding and periods when it is contracting. There will be times when everything is great, and times when nothing seems to go well. It's during these challenging times that your personal commitment to helping the vertical, along with an empathetic understanding, will pave the way for delivering exceptional value to your clients, establishing your agency as a reliable partner through thick and thin.

At the end of the day, it's about being genuinely useful. In Joe Polish's words, "Being useful begins with being caring. It takes two parts: being aware of other people's needs, wants, pains, and problems, and then offering a solution. In doing so, be an active listener, empathize, and don't overwhelm, and give solutions that are simple to execute."[21]

Support When They Need It

At my last agency when COVID hit, we lowered or completely waived our monthly fees for clients who were impacted by the slowing economy. We also took significant efforts to connect with them one-on-one, so that we could help guide them through the uncertain times.

Yes, our revenue sustained a short-term hit, but this was one of those defining moments where the well-being and survival of our clients' businesses was our top priority. This client-first approach came back to us in spades as we exited the pandemic: client goodwill was at an all-time high.

TAPPING INTO PREEXISTING CONNECTIONS

A connection to a vertical market can often come from personal or familial experiences, which may naturally cultivate empathy towards clients within that sector. Here are a few examples:

- **ServiceTitan**: Valued at $9.5 billion,[22] this software company for home services contractors was founded by individuals whose parents worked in home services.
- **Toms Shoes**: With a brand value of $400 million,[23] Toms Shoes was launched by the child of an orthopedic surgeon.
- **Blaze Pizza**: The daughter of the Wetzel's Pretzels founder spearheaded this $347[24] million fast-casual pizza chain, carrying forward a family legacy in the food industry with a fresh perspective.

These personal connections to a specific market can foster genuine empathy and a desire to make a positive impact. However, empathy can also come from other sources.

- Chris Yano, founder of RYNO Strategic Solutions, a successful eight-figure digital marketing agency targeting HVAC and other home services businesses, felt more comfortable around blue-collar workers, leading to him to focus his agency on the trades.
- Alex Membrillo, founder of Cardinal Digital Marketing, an eight-figure agency targeting multi-location medical practices, chose to focus on healthcare due to his love for helping others.
- Carman Pirie, cofounder of Kula Partners, a premier HubSpot Partner specializing in the manufacturing sector, felt an affinity with the people and communities that manufacturing companies support.

These examples underscore that while personal or familial connections to a vertical can drive success, they aren't prerequisites. A genuine concern for your clients' challenges, a comfort level with your client base, and a desire to help can also foster a meaningful connection to a vertical, setting the foundation for long-term success.

"I love being in the space that I'm passionate about. If I was niching in some other industry that I didn't really care anything about, I might not be as excited about it."

LEANNE PRESSLY, founder and CEO of Stitchcraft[25]

THE PRACTICAL VALUE OF EMPATHY

Seth Godin's insight "Don't find customers for your products, find products for your customers" encapsulates a client-centric approach. Instead of pushing a preconceived service, an agency should understand its clientele deeply, tailoring its offerings to meet their specific needs. This is where empathy becomes a linchpin for success, especially when you're focusing on a particular vertical market. Here's how empathy translates into tangible business wins.

- **Differentiation:** By investing emotional effort to understand and meet your clients' needs, you set yourself apart from competitors who are only transaction oriented.
- **Improved Communication:** Clients who feel like you care will communicate with you more often, especially

when they feel things aren't going well. That gives you a chance to nip problems in the bud.

- **Stronger Relationships:** Building trust through empathetic interactions leads to a foundation where clients are less likely to micromanage or second-guess your recommendations.
- **Grace under Fire:** Mistakes are inevitable, but when they occur, clients who know you care are more likely to respond with understanding and patience.
- **Word of Mouth:** Exceeding clients' expectations through empathetic service not only retains their loyalty but also improves the likelihood of them recommending your services to others within their vertical.

By aligning your business ethos with empathy, you create fertile ground for long-term client relationships, better communication, and a robust reputation within your vertical, which ultimately increases your business success.

HOW TO EMPATHIZE WITH YOUR VERTICAL MARKET

Here are five things you can do to connect deeply with your vertical market.

1. **See beyond the Transaction**
   Recognize that your client represents more than just economic value. They are humans with aspirations,

challenges, and emotions. Just like you, they have hopes and fears tied to their business success.

2. **Discover Their Why**
Delve into the motivations driving the founders or senior leaders you work with. Ask questions like:

- Why did you start your company?
- What does success look like to you?
- How does your business contribute to your life, family, or community?

3. **Express Genuine Curiosity**
Authentic curiosity can't be faked; if it's forced, it comes across as disingenuous. Engage in conversations that allow you to better understand their industry and the unique challenges they face.

4. **Engage in Active Listening**
When clients share their experiences or concerns, listen attentively. Reflect on their words and respond thoughtfully, demonstrating that you value their perspective.

5. **Be Ready to Adapt**
Based on what you learn, be willing to adapt your strategies to better serve your clients. This shows that you not only understand their needs but are committed to meeting them.

Deep Specialization Pro Tip: If you find yourself avoiding this type of inquiry, think deeply about whether your vertical aligns with your interests and values. Engaging in a vertical that resonates with you personally can naturally foster a deeper connection with your clients.

"If I'm going to be doing this business stuff, it's got to be something I'm passionate about. I can only get so passionate about digital marketing. So, who are we doing it for? What's the bigger mission?"

LUKE EGGEBRAATEN[26], founder of Phaser Marketing

In the next chapter, I'll walk you through the four-step process for selecting the best vertical for your agency.

CHAPTER TAKEAWAYS

- Long-term success is rooted in genuinely caring about clients, their challenges, and their successes.
- Support your clients during tough times, and they will respond with loyalty.
- While personal or familial connections to a vertical can drive success, they are not prerequisites.
- Embracing empathy sets your agency apart from competitors.
- Success with Deep Specialization requires going beyond mere transactions; it's about passion, purpose, and the broader mission of whom you serve and why.

Chapter 5
The Four-Step Process

"If you aim at nothing, you will hit it every time."

ZIG ZIGLAR, author, salesman, and motivational speaker[27]

There are four steps in the process for identifying the best vertical market for your agency:

Step 1: Gather your client data.
Step 2: Identify three verticals.
Step 3: Score the verticals.
Step 4: Validate the market.

⊙ Completing these four steps can take up to three hours. Think of these three hours as both an investment and insurance policy, preventing the costly mistake of choosing the wrong vertical market for your agency.

The only things you'll need to get started are your client data, an internet browser, and a hot cup of tea to help keep you focused.

I recommend reading through the entire four-step process before beginning. Then open the companion workbook, go back through the chapter a second time, and do the exercises. This way, you'll understand the process before you start playing with the dials and knobs.

STEP 1: GATHER YOUR CLIENT DATA

Use your client financial and sales data to help identify a handful of client vertical markets with which you've had success. Here's a list of the client data you'll need to gather and organize:

- Total number of clients by vertical
- Average client annual revenue per client vertical
- Average client retention by vertical (in months)

Start by grouping your current clients into verticals.

For example, let's say you have a total of 33 clients. When you group them by vertical market, you learn that you have nine law firms, nine auto dealers, five retail businesses, four dentists, three chiropractors, and three hospitals.

If this is the first time you're grouping your clients into vertical markets, you may need some help with naming your client verticals. If you get stuck, remember that there is no right way to choose vertical names for these groups. Use common sense, and group your clients into verticals based on what is most practical. Don't overthink it!

For example, let's say you have a variety of dental professionals as clients, including general dentists, pedodontists (dentists for kids), orthodontists, and periodontists. You could either group them as a single vertical, Dentists, or you could break out each type of dentist into separate verticals in the worksheet. You are the best person to make the call on this. You can always rework the groupings as you complete this process if you realize that your original organization isn't optimal.

Deep Specialization Pro Tip: If you need help assigning vertical names to your clients, here's a reference list you can use: naics.com/naics-drilldown-table.

If your current client list is light on vertical market data, you may also want to include client data from previous clients.

Once you've named and grouped your current client list into vertical markets, it's time to add three pieces of client data.

- Total number of clients by vertical
- Average annual revenue by vertical
- Average client retention by vertical (in months)

STEP 2: IDENTIFY THREE VERTICALS

Now ask yourself: Which vertical markets stand out?

Seeing this client data for the first time may cause some verticals to jump out, or it may not. (And if not, that's okay!) Either way, now's the time to select three verticals to progress through the remaining two steps in this process.

You may choose three verticals based on your tangible client metrics. Or you may decide to choose a vertical because you have a particular interest in it despite not having supportive client data. Either way is fine. Just choose (up to) three.

STEP 3: SCORE THE VERTICALS

Now that you've isolated three verticals, score these verticals through a qualitative lens for fit. This step helps ensure that you'll be choosing a vertical market that is not only financially strong but that aligns with your company strategy and preferred market dynamics.

Rate the three verticals based on 17 qualitative measures using a rating scale from 1 to 10, where 10 is an Enthusiastic Yes! and 1 is a Big No.

Agency Experience

- Does our sales team like selling to buyers in this vertical?
- Does our client success team like helping clients in this vertical?
- Do I like working with this vertical?

Company and Market Strategy

- Does this vertical fit with my vision for the company?
- Does this vertical fit with our service and product road map?
- Do we have a competitive advantage in this vertical?
- Is our agency uniquely positioned within the vertical?
- Is this vertical relatively recession proof?

Vertical Dynamics

- Is the revenue greater than $1 million?
- Is there a close-knit community?
- Is there industry jargon?
- Is the market growing, on the rise?
- Are professional requirements needed?
- Are there multiple associations and conferences?
- Do we have a personal or familial connection?
- Do we have a professional connection?
- Does our agency have existing recognition in the vertical?

Agency Experience

Does our sales team like selling to buyers in this vertical?

After 25 years of operating in and leading sales teams, I've learned that a sales team always prefers selling to a particular type of buyer when they know the product or service they're selling will genuinely deliver on its promise.

Salespeople are human too. They operate best with confidence and momentum, and the optimal way to get a salesperson to be a top producer is to give them a great product or service to sell that produces happy clients.

Unless you're 100% certain which verticals your sales team prefers selling to, ask your head of sales to rate each vertical with you. It might also be worth interviewing a couple of other members of the sales team (admins, frontline sellers, etc.) for additional context and feedback.

Does our client success team like helping clients in this vertical?

Like sales teams, client success teams enjoy working with a particular type of client: happy clients. Happy clients receive the service and results they bought, and then some.

By contrast, there's nothing worse than regularly getting calls from upset clients who feel they're not getting what they were sold.

While you may already know which verticals they prefer serving, if you aren't 100% certain, talk directly with your client success team leaders and ask them how they would rate working with clients by vertical. You can also interview members of your frontline client service team for their perspectives.

Do I like working with this vertical?

This is your agency, so you're the best person to judge the qualitative nature of working with your clients. Ask yourself: Do I like working with these people? Do I deeply care about their success? Does their success align with my values and interests?

Why does this matter? Because empathy and care for your clients is a critical factor in both their success and yours.

"I was actually finding that I could charge reasonable rates and do great work for the [nonprofit sector] and be doing work that I believed in."

SARAH DURHAM, founder of Big Duck

Company and Market Strategy

Does this vertical fit with my vision for the company?

Your company vision represents what the future holds for your agency. What goals do you want to achieve? What impact do you want to make? How many employees do you want to have? How many clients are you serving? How much revenue and profit do you want to make? How much freedom do you want in your business and life? And so on.

With these factors in mind, based on your subjective opinion, does focusing on this vertical fit your vision for the company?

Does this vertical fit with our service and product road map?

Ask yourself: Does this vertical have a problem I can already expertly solve?

For example, Scorpion started with attorneys and then expanded into home services. Why?

- They are local service businesses, just like attorneys.
- They get leads and jobs from the internet, just like attorneys.
- They have high search volumes and large budgets, just like attorneys.
- They need pretty much everything attorneys do when it comes to marketing.

- Plus, Scorpion had a few home services clients who were very happy and getting great results.

Do we have a competitive advantage in this vertical?

Competitive advantages include:

- Deep understanding of the nuances, customer behavior, pain points, and emerging trends
- Specialized tools, software, or processes
- Strategic relationships
- Specialized talent or team members
- Case studies with influential brands

Is our agency uniquely positioned within the vertical?

Are we already seen as a leader in the vertical? Do we have key relationships with the influential thought leaders in the vertical? Are we known for our unique technology or approach?

Is this vertical relatively recession proof?

Looking back on the recent COVID-19 pandemic, certain industries and verticals did okay, and others didn't do so well. Industries that did well include plumbing, home gym equipment, delivery services, and cleaning services. Industries that didn't do well include airlines, hotels, and restaurants. While any industry is susceptible to getting hit with short-term recessionary pressures, some verticals are more vulnerable than others.

When it comes to your vertical markets, do your

research and try to determine how susceptible they are to a recession.

Vertical Dynamics

We covered vertical dynamics in Chapter 3 with a table of the nine preferred dynamics. Flip back to that section to review it, and then score each vertical on those dynamics.

Add Them Up!

Now add up the scores across your three vertical markets. The higher the total number, the greater the likelihood the vertical is a good fit for your business.

STEP 4: VALIDATE THE MARKET

The last step in this process is to validate that the vertical you choose will meet your business growth aspirations. Simply put, does the vertical market have enough revenue opportunity to justify focusing your agency on it?

We'll confirm this by looking at market data for the vertical and applying this formula:

$$\text{TAM x 20\% x 3\% x average revenue per client}$$
$$= \text{estimated revenue in 3 years}$$

I prepared a quick video tutorial on how to get free information on industry growth trends and market sizing from IBISWorld in the online workbook. Download the free companion workbook at AnyoneNotEveryone.com to watch it.

Total Addressable Market (TAM)

The total addressable market, or TAM, is the total number of businesses that exist today in the vertical market that you could sell your services to.

You may already be very familiar with the market, but now is the time to discover the actual number of businesses that exist in the vertical. Arthur Nielsen Sr., founder of the Nielsen Company, said, "If you can put a number on it, then you know something."[28] And he's right!

For example, a quick search for dentists, personal injury attorneys, and plumbing franchises revealed that in the U.S. there are:

- 191,497 dental practices
- 64,331 personal injury attorneys
- 2,984 plumbing franchise brands

Use the most accurate number you can for the TAM for your specific niche. For example, you may not be targeting all law firms in the U.S.; you might want to target personal injury attorneys. In this case, you'd use the total number of personal injury attorneys as your addressable market size.

How Small Is Too Small?

How small of a total addressable market is too small? Author and positioning expert David C. Baker recommends choosing verticals with more than 2,000 businesses.[29] If yours has fewer than that, then it might not be worth pursuing.

In addition to the number of businesses, pay attention to the average revenue that businesses in the vertical make. If it's less than $1 million, think carefully about whether they'll be able to afford your services.

Multiply TAM by 20%

We're going to assume that only 20% of the TAM will be a good fit for your services. It's the Pareto principle, an 80/20 split. The percentage could be much higher, but we're taking a conservative approach. We'll call this your Pareto addressable market.

Multiply by 3%

This 3% represents a semi-conservative expectation of your share of the market in three years. In other words, by focusing on this one vertical market, in three years, you should expect to have around 3% of your Pareto addressable market as clients.

Multiply by Average Revenue per Client

The best revenue number to use here is the average revenue your vertical client spends with you per year. If you don't have this figure available, make your best guess at what it would be.

The Result
The result of this equation is the amount of revenue you'll earn in three years from this vertical market. Looking at the number, ask yourself: Does this number meet my expectations and goals?

If the answer is yes, then you have validated your vertical market.

If the answer is no, then you can either further refine your vertical market by adjusting the total addressable market size and/or the revenue per client, or you can run the same analysis on one of your backup vertical markets.

An Example of Market Validation
I recently took a strategic integrated communications agency through this process. We identified hospital systems as a potential vertical market. The research shows there are 2,466 hospital systems in the U.S., and their average annual revenue for a hospital systems client is $150,000.

Let's apply this data to the equation:

$$2,466 \times 20\% \times 3\% \times \$150,000 = \$2,219,400$$

My client's response when I asked if that revenue target worked for them was "It sure does!"

Your Turn: Three-Day Challenge

Now it's time for you to jump online and use the workbook to help you identify your vertical market. I invite you to take the Focus Finder Three-Day Challenge:

- Share this four-step process with your team, along with why you're doing it.
- Gather your current client data and go through Steps 1 to 4 within the next three days.

In the next chapter, I'll introduce the next phase: studying the psychology behind what motivates your vertical market buyer.

| **CHAPTER SUMMARY**

- There are four steps to identify your ideal vertical market: gather your client data, identify three verticals, score them, and validate the market.
- Agency experience matters. Sales teams prefer selling to clients they believe in, and client success teams prefer working with happy clients.
- It's essential for agency owners to personally enjoy working with the chosen vertical.
- Your chosen vertical should align with your agency's vision, product, and service road map.

Step 2

Study Your Vertical Market Buyer

DEEP SPECIALIZATION

Choose the Perfect
Vertical Market

Match Your Message
to Your Vertical

Build the Team

✓ —— 2 —— 3 —— 4 —— 5

Study Your Vertical
Market Buyer

Plan Your
Campaigns

Chapter 6

Get into the Mind of Your Vertical Buyer

> "You'll learn more in a day talking to customers than a week of brainstorming, a month of watching competitors, or a year of market research."
>
> Aaron Levie, CEO of Box[30]

N ow that you have identified a vertical market to target, let's talk about how to get into their heads so your marketing stands out.

When it comes to marketing, it's excruciatingly easy to waste money. The biggest contributing factor to this waste is a lack of relevancy. Buyers ignore marketing that is irrelevant to them.

The reason is oversaturation. Each of us is exposed to 5,000 marketing messages per day.[31] Our brains are wired to screen out 100% of the messages that don't directly speak to us—our needs, desires, and fears.

For example, let's say you're a plastic surgeon who recently launched a private practice and you are looking for new patients. You see these two advertisements from two different digital marketing agencies. Which advertisement headline would you be more likely to notice?

Just Launched Your Plastic Surgery Practice?
We Help Fill Your New Practice with Great Patients

Just Launched a New Business?
We Help Fill Your Business with Great Customers

The first headline is obviously more relevant and would catch your eye.

You want your vertical buyers to not only notice your marketing but be magnetized by it. You do this by first understanding their needs, desires, and fears. Then you communicate to them in a way that reflects that understanding while tipping them off that you're an insider to their world.

Doing so requires you to do the emotional labor of understanding your vertical buyer's specific context, what they care about, what motivates them, and even what scares them.

INTERVIEW YOUR VERTICAL CLIENTS

It's tempting to assume that you already know the inner workings of the buyers in your vertical. It is especially tempting if you've been serving them for an extended period. However, the more intentional you can be about improving your understanding of your buyers, and either validating or disputing the assumptions you have about them and their preferences, the better you can market to them in a way that breaks through the noise.

There are many ways to research your buyers, including conducting surveys, doing focus groups, or observing them using your product. But those methods leave you with a surface-level understanding due to the lack of real-time interaction and the ability to ask follow-up questions.

The best way to truly understand clients and their motivations is to interview them one-on-one.

By following the specific framework I'm about to share with you, you'll gain a new understanding about your buyer that exponentially strengthens your marketing.

Client interviews are widely discussed, yet rarely executed by most teams. But for committed founders, this is not busy work. In fact, real revelations emerge from these dialogues. Take the experience of the GIFT•OLOGY Group, a firm that excels in keeping clients in the forefront of minds. "We never saw ourselves as an agency," founder John Ruhlin admits. "More like gifting experts, executive assistants, maybe concierges." However, their tailored customer interviews unveiled a startling truth: "Our clients were their own biggest impediment." Repeatedly, they encountered the same refrain: "We know we should be investing more in relationships, but we've never got around to it because this excuse or that." Desire existed, yet urgency did not. "That's when we recognized our role in enforcing accountability," John explains. "It's akin to having a 5 a.m. gym buddy. You might skip solo workouts, but you'd never let your partner down. We became the gym partner."

What Does a Successful Client Interview Look Like?

Client interviews aren't a social conversation with your favorite client. They also aren't opportunities to confirm your existing assumptions or gather opinions about your ideas.

Instead, a client interview is a guided and structured conversation designed to uncover the often hidden beliefs, behaviors, and goals of your buyer. The conversation is designed to challenge your assumptions and biases while providing you with the opportunity to learn actionable insights.

Once you've completed seven to ten of these interviews, you'll easily identify patterns in client responses, which you can turn into insights to use in marketing. More on that soon.

Types of Client Interviews

Smart agency founders and their teams regularly interview their clients across all the stages of their clients' life cycles. Here's a high-level overview of the types of client interviews.

Type of Client Interview	Target Audience	Designed to Understand
Buyer Journey	Individuals who make the buying decisions	How and why they buy
Win/Loss	Clients who went through your sales process	Sales effectiveness
Churn / Win Back	Ex-clients	Why they left
User Interviews	Users of your product or service	How they use your product or service

For the purposes of this book, we're going to primarily focus on the Buyer Journey client interview.

Deep Specialization Pro Tip: Don't cram two or more types of interviews into a single 30-minute session, as it's too much to cover and you'll end up only scratching the surface. Instead, dedicate the time to one type of client interview, the Buyer Journey, so you can get a deep look into your buyer's beliefs, behaviors, and goals.

Three Steps to Successful Buyer Journey Client Interviews

⏱ This entire three-step process, including the client calls and compiling the analysis and takeaways, shouldn't take more than ten hours over two to three weeks. If you're going over ten hours, you're probably overdoing it.

STEP 1: INTERVIEW PREP

Setting Objectives and Outcomes

This process begins with the end in mind, just like constructing a building: you wouldn't start without a clear blueprint. That's why defining your research objectives and desired outcomes is crucial. The first step is to sketch out your plans for what you want to achieve from your client interviews.

Defining your objectives and outcomes organizes your thoughts, improves the quality of your questions, and helps ensure the clients you're interviewing have a good experience.

Your **primary objective** is to understand **how** and **why** clients in your vertical buy from you. Your **primary outcome** is to complete the client interview section in the companion workbook. You'll use this later to refine your agency's positioning and messaging.

If you don't have seven to ten clients to interview in your vertical, invite your best-fit clients in any vertical. While this will limit what you learn about your vertical itself, you will certainly gain insights about your clients' buying journey, what they value about working with you, and why they stay with you.

What You're Looking to Uncover in the Buyer Journey Interview

There are five key buying criteria you're looking to uncover in the client interviews:

1. The biggest challenges your client had with the former solution
2. Their rational and emotional consequences of doing it the old way
3. What caused them to finally make a switch
4. How and where they researched alternatives to their current solution
5. Why they bought your services

Insights on these five key buying criteria will give you more clarity on your vertical's buying process, which you can later use in your marketing, positioning, and messaging.

Here's a breakdown of each.

1. The biggest challenges your client had with the former solution

Goal: To learn two or three of their big challenges.

Why this is important: There is a high likelihood that the big challenges your vertical clients faced before hiring you will be the same challenges your future vertical clients are currently facing. Knowing what these challenges are and using them in your marketing will help increase your relevancy and build insider trust.

For example, let's say you're an SEO agency, and your vertical is family law attorneys. Through the buyer journey interviews, you learn that prior to working with you, the common challenge your family law attorney clients faced was spending a lot of money on SEO that only yielded low-value child support cases from it. In this example, only getting low-value child support cases is the challenge.

2. Their rational and emotional consequences of doing it the old way

Goal: To understand the true cost of the problem.

Why this is important: Accurately articulating your vertical buyer's problem in your marketing, along with understanding the rational and emotional consequences they face, communicates that you are a specialist in their world, creating deeper relevancy and trust with buyers.

Continuing with the example above, the consequences of working with the family law firm's previous agency were fewer high-value divorce cases, wasted marketing dollars, and missed opportunities. Further, they saw competing firms get more prominence online, close bigger cases, and get more positive reviews. This left the family law attorney angry, frustrated, and feeling hopeless.

3. What caused them to finally make a switch

Goal: To learn the trigger that transformed the issue from a yeah-we'll-deal-with-it-someday problem into a bleeding-neck priority.[32]

Why this is important: Communicating this breaking point in your marketing declares that you get them *and* that you know how to solve their problem. It gets your future buyers leaning in and saying, "Hey, how did you know that?"

Continuing with the example above, you learn that what caused your current family law firm clients to switch was their account manager at the old agency who seemed emotionally disconnected and uninterested in helping. The straw that broke the camel's back? When they went three months without a new case from their SEO and were met with consistent indifference from their account manager. They realized the situation wasn't going to change and they needed to start shopping around for a better agency ASAP.

4. How and where they researched alternatives to their current solution

Goal: To understand what they did the moment they decided to find a new agency, and then the next moment, and the next ... all the way until they decided to sign a contract with you. What were their steps, where did they go, and who did they talk to?

Why this is important: Knowing your buyer's journey gives you clues as to where your future buyers will go to find you, trust you, and ultimately buy from you. This road map will greatly influence which marketing channels you invest in (e.g., conferences, podcasting, PPC, thought leadership, etc.).

Continuing with the example above, you learn that once your family law attorney client decided to make a change, the first thing they did was go on Google to see which of their competitors appear on the first page of results. Then they tried to discover which agencies those competitors use. They then asked attorneys in their professional networks and groups which agencies they use and recommend. Next, they listened to law firm marketing podcasts to hear what influencers, thought leaders, and their peers have to say. Last, they went to review sites like Clutch.co to read reviews from other attorneys using your agency.

While the actual buying process isn't always this linear, what's important is to find the patterns in how your current vertical clients find their next agency.

5. Why they bought your services
Goal: To uncover the specific attributes, benefits, and features that caused your vertical clients to trust and ultimately choose you out of the hundreds, if not thousands, of potential options.[33]

Why this is important: It's more than likely that your future vertical clients will choose you for the same attributes, benefits, and features that appealed to your current clients. When you know what those are specifically, you can use them in your sales and marketing to cut through the noise, communicate relevancy, and build trust.

To wrap up the example, you learn that your family law attorney clients chose you because you share the same client-first values as they do, you're willing to build a custom SEO strategy for them and take a hands-on approach to optimizing their current site, and you have a ton of positive reviews from other attorneys. Also mentioned were the relevant case studies on your website, having credible law firms as clients, and that you include intake coaching with your marketing services.

The Seven Best Questions to Ask
Your goal with client interviews is to solicit buyers' needs, desires, and fears—not to confirm an assumption or bias that you hope is true.

As Chris Voss writes in *Never Split the Difference*, "Your goal at the outset is to extract and observe as much information as possible. Which, by the way, is one of the reasons that really smart people often have trouble being negotiators—they're so smart they think they don't have anything to discover."[34]

While a client interview is not a hostage negotiation, it's easy to slip into the mindset of "I know this thing to be true; I'm just talking to my client to confirm."

Instead, go into the interviews with an open mind, eager to learn the facts. Your questions should be open-ended and non-leading so you don't get false-positive answers that aren't helpful. For example, compare: "How did you manage new employee training before partnering with us?" to "Was the way you managed new employees outdated before partnering with us?"

In other words, no leading the witness.

Here's a short list of questions that you can use to solicit the five key buying criteria mentioned above. Feel free to customize them as needed to suit your voice.

- How did you manage [problem we solve] before partnering with us? Walk me through what that was like.
- What were the biggest challenges with [the way they used to manage the problem]?
- What were the consequences of each of those challenges? [Ask about the consequences for each challenge.]

- When and why did these challenges become a priority to solve?
- What actions did you take to solve these challenges and ultimately find us? [Other ways to ask this are "What did you do?" or "Where did you go? or "Who did you talk to?"]
- What made you trust our agency? What made you comfortable?
- Why did you ultimately choose to go with us?

Notice that I listed seven client interview questions. You can add more, but try to keep it under 15 questions total. Allocate three to four minutes for each big topic question, with time for follow-up questions. The follow-up questions usually reveal key insights. Consider this example dialogue:

Original question:	What challenges were you facing with doing everything in-house?
Client:	*We rarely posted on social media.*
First follow-up question:	That's interesting that you said you rarely posted. Could you expand on that?

Client:	*Sure, we would post maybe once per month. There were times when we went two or three months without posting at all.*
Second follow-up question:	What prevented you from posting more often?

Discussion Guide

An important benefit of documenting your questions before jumping into the client interviews is it ensures you're asking each of your clients the same core set of questions. That way, you'll be able to compare their various responses, making it easier to find commonalities, insights, and patterns.

Your documented master list of questions is called your discussion guide. The companion workbook includes a free discussion guide template, along with the seven client interview questions listed above.

Setting Up Interviews with Vertical Clients

Pull up a list of your vertical clients and identify those who you think would be open to giving you 30 to 45 minutes of their time. Not every one of your vertical clients will be able to do this, so I recommend creating an initial list of 15 clients that you feel comfortable reaching out to. These could be clients that you personally dealt with in the sales process, clients who actively engage with your client success teams, or clients who have seen outsized results from working with you.

You're initially aiming for seven to ten interviews. Research has shown that once you hit around ten completed interviews, you'll hit saturation: you gain relatively few new insights with each additional client interview.

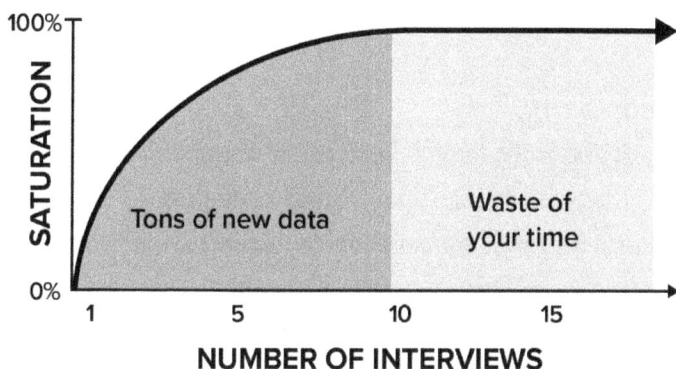

Deep Specialization Pro Tip: Schedule two initial interviews before scheduling the rest. These pilot interviews will give you an opportunity to try out the questions and make improvements to the process and discussion guide as needed. Then you can proceed with the remainder of the interviews.

How you reach out and invite your clients to an interview has an impact on the likelihood of them saying yes. Unfortunately, there really isn't much of an obvious upside to the client by spending time with you and answering questions that will lead to you getting more clients.

You'll need to tap into the goodwill that you've built over the life of the relationship with these clients. Sure, you can offer them an incentive of some sort, but this may backfire if they're simply motivated to get the incentive and not genuinely interested in helping you and your company become more successful.

Here's a sample script that you can customize for your client outreach:

> *Dear [client],*
>
> *It's been too long! I hope you're doing well!*
>
> *I wanted to see if you would be willing to have a chat with [me / someone on my team]. We're seeking to better understand a little more about how and why our best clients chose to partner with [our company].*
>
> *I'm interested in hearing about your experience, so I thought I'd reach out and see if you'd consider it.*
>
> *The 25-to-30-minute call is over Zoom and super casual.*
>
> *It's totally fine to say no, but if you're up for it, just shoot back a yes/thumbs-up, and we'll get it booked.*
>
> *Thanks for your consideration!*
>
> *Best,*
>
> *[Your Name]*

The Best Person to Interview for a Buyer Journey

Your day-to-day contact is not necessarily the person who was the decision-maker in the buying process.

For example, let's say you're selling Facebook advertising services, and your vertical is chain restaurants with more than ten locations. The primary person who works with your team is the restaurant brand's marketing manager, Sally. She knows the ins and outs of every aspect of your service, is a true power user, and is a vocal advocate for your brand.

Even though Sally's wildly familiar with your service, if she's not directly involved with the buying process, she won't be very helpful to interview for the buyer's journey. She may, however, be a great candidate for a user interview.

STEP 2: DURING THE INTERVIEWS

Here are some best practices for a smooth client interview.

Have a Conversation

Nothing creates canned, unhelpful responses quicker than if your client feels you have an agenda or you're trying to get something from them. The best way to establish a friendly, conversational tone is right when you open the call.

Here's an opener I use that tends to put the client immediately at ease.

Welcome to the call, [first name]. Thanks for hopping on with me; it really means a lot to us. I asked you to hop on with me because I'm interested in learning more about the period right before you hired our agency, leading up to when you chose us.

The plan for the call is I'm going to ask you a few open-ended questions, and you can respond however you want, but just know there are no right or wrong answers. We're just looking for a better understanding of your experience at that time.

It should take only about 20 to 30 minutes. Sound good? Do you have any initial questions for me?

Use the Discussion Guide, Be an Active Listener, and Ask Follow-up Questions

It's commonplace for a client to be cautious or unsure. They don't want to disappoint you, and they may be eager to tell you what you want to hear, in order to please.

A great technique for transforming a client from cautious to trusting and open is to be an active listener. Active listening means mirroring back what you hear the client say. It communicates that you're genuinely listening and value what they're saying. It also gives them a bit more confidence to open up and go deeper.

Deep Specialization Pro Tip: Study your discussion guide before you hop into the interview. Know it inside and out so you can be present and natural on the call. Alternatively, you can position your discussion guide near the camera on your screen. That way you can look directly at the person you're interviewing but still refer to your questions (without looking at your notebook or a separate monitor).

During the interview, use phrases like "So let me feed this back to you to confirm I get what you're saying: [say what they said]. Did I get that right?" Often, they'll confirm and expand on what they said, or you'll uncover an opportunity to ask a follow-up question.

Record the Call Using a Real-Time Transcription Service
Recording your client interview calls using a real-time transcription service accomplishes three things:

- You'll have an audio archive of exactly what the client said. You can review the verbatim discussion as it actually unfolded.
- You can relax into the conversation and be present with your client, instead of trying to write down everything said.
- You can copy and paste their answers directly into your discussion guide for further review.

Close the Interview with an Invitation
It's likely your client will continue thinking about the conversation after the interview is over and will remember something useful. As you're wrapping up your call, offer them the opportunity to email you if they think of anything else they may have missed.

Then thank them for their time and for being a great client.

STEP 3: AFTER THE INTERVIEWS

With your seven to ten buyer journey client interviews completed, it's time to organize the responses and capture new insights.

Organize

- Open a blank document and title it "Buyer Journey Client Response Master." (A template is available in the companion workbook.)
  - Copy/paste the questions from your discussion guide into the document.
  - Pull up the call transcripts and copy/paste the verbatim responses from each client below the respective questions and label which client said it.
- Read through each question and response. Bold or highlight the key phrases that hit on any of the following:
  - Emotions: These are feelings like excitement, frustration, apathy, indifference, etc.
  - Behaviors: These are the frequent activities or actions the person engages in.
  - Problems: These are any specific challenges or pains they talk about that you didn't bring up.
  - Solutions: These are ideas your client might present or that they've already used to solve a problem.
  - Surprises: These are the random nuggets that make you go, "Huh."

- Look for similar themes, phrases, and words being used across each response. Broader patterns and threads will connect the experiences.
- Look for mentions of other agencies who they considered before choosing you. These competitors will be worth noting for potential further research.
- Do:
  - Let the responses you gathered guide the insights.
  - Look for anything that progressed their decisions.
  - Look for anything that gives you insights about their motivation.
- Don't:
  - Cherry-pick answers to confirm a bias or assumption.

Capture Insights

- Use the Buyer Journey Summary and Takeaways template in the companion workbook to document your insights and takeaways from your client interviews. Or create your own using the five buying criteria you were looking to uncover in the client interviews:
  - The biggest challenges our clients had with their old solution
  - Their rational and emotional consequences of doing it the old way
  - What caused them to finally make a switch
  - How and where they researched alternatives
  - Why they bought our services over all the other options available to them

- Have both this document and the Buyer Journey Client Response Master document up on your screens and visible, if possible.
- Summarize the key themes, insights, and takeaways for each buying criteria.

What Success Looks Like

You are done with this process when you can confidently identify at least one insight in each of the five buying criteria for your vertical.

Now that you have an intimate understanding of how and why your vertical buyers buy from you, it's time to work on your Deep Specialization positioning and differentiation.

CHAPTER TAKEAWAYS

- Understanding the specific needs, desires, and fears of your buyers is essential to creating effective marketing messages and strategies that resonate in your vertical.
- Marketing efforts often fail due to a lack of relevancy and to oversaturation.
- A marketing message tailored to your vertical buyer's specific needs, desires, and fears is likely to capture their attention and resonate with them.
- To gain a deep understanding of vertical buyers, shed your assumptions and actively seek genuine insights into what they care about, their motivations, and fears.
- The best way to capture these insights and gain a more nuanced understanding is through one-on-one client interviews focusing on the buyer journey.

Chapter 7

Know Your Vertical Competition

"Study the methods of your competitors
and do the exact opposite."

DAVID OGILVY, founder of Ogilvy & Mather,
and the "Father of Advertising"[35]

N obody hires your agency in a vacuum; they choose you from an array of competing options.

Why evaluate your competitors? HubSpot research found 90% of marketers report positive impacts on their business from using competitive research as part of their strategy.[36]

The argument for focusing on your competitors is you'll stay on top of how others in your category are innovating their services, positioning their brands, and satisfying their clients.

The argument against focusing too heavily on your

competition is it takes your eye off the most important aspect of your business: your clients. You know, the ones paying you to solve their problems.

Focusing too much on your competitors can cause you to make reactive strategic decisions, such as launching a new service line or changing contract terms. These changes might prove unproductive because they aren't grounded in solving real problems for your clients.

Just because your competition launches a new feature doesn't mean that you should too.

The line I take is that it's healthy to study your competitors so you can better understand the psychology of how and why your clients buy from you as well as how and why they buy from the alternatives. Armed with this information, you can make better decisions about how to position and market your agency services in your vertical.

Additionally, the competitive research you do in this chapter will inform the work in the following chapters.

DEFINING YOUR VERTICAL COMPETITORS

Knowing who your competitors are likely to be, as well as how they're positioning their agency services, products, and solutions, helps you experience what your buyers do when shopping for a new agency.

Your vertical competitors are:

- Businesses that clients choose when they don't choose you
- Businesses your clients go to when they leave you

But it's even worse than that. Your biggest competitor probably isn't who you think it is. No, it's not the company across the virtual street selling the same service as yours but packaged differently.

Your biggest competitor is when your buyer chooses *not* to change what they're currently doing. In other words, it's when your buyer chooses to maintain the status quo, even if they're literally suffering daily by staying put.

Authors Matthew Dixon and Ted McKenna found that anywhere between 40% and 60% of deals today end up stalled in "no decision" limbo.[37]

Just like the folks sticking to their traditional cable subscriptions when there are better online streaming options, these buyers avoid changing because they don't want the inconvenience and effort of making a change.

The problem is that your buyers, like all of us humans, are not quite fully rational beings. We fear change because it means stepping into the unknown. For many, it creates a fear of losing control and a possibility of failure.

We have a cognitive bias called loss aversion, which says the pain of losing is psychologically twice as powerful as the pleasure of gaining.[38] So, what do we do? We stay in the comfort of the status quo. As the saying goes, "Better the devil you know than the devil you don't."

But it's possible to overcome the status quo and beat competitors. Here are some success stories:

Company	Status Quo Competitor
Slack	Sending interoffice email
Airbnb	Staying in hotels
Netflix	Going to the video rental store

Your buyer's status quo is a competitor you'll need to get good at beating, especially if you don't want to rely solely on inbound leads to grow your business. Who wants to build a business that doesn't have control over its growth? (More on outbound marketing in Chapter 14.)

THE THREE-STEP RESEARCH PROCESS

◉ This entire three-step process, including the research and analysis, shouldn't take more than three hours to complete.

- Step One: Identify Your Competitors
- Step Two: Research Your Competitors
- Step Three: Document Your Findings

STEP 1: IDENTIFY YOUR COMPETITORS

If you're the founder of your agency, you're probably familiar with your competitors. If you have any doubts, ask the folks on your sales team (if you have one) where your prospective clients go when they don't choose you. Next, ask your client success teams where your clients go when they leave you. This quick research should give you a healthy list of competitors.

If you need more ideas, hop onto Google and search using keywords related to your vertical and your agency services. For example, if you're a content marketing agency targeting higher education, you could search terms like "content marketing for higher education" or "content marketing for colleges." Look for agencies that are thought leaders and rank highly in the organic search results. Your current clients are another reliable source. Reach out to a few and ask who they consider to be your competition.

You only need five competitors for now. At least three of them need to be vertical specialist agencies and the other two can be generalist agencies.

Vertical specialist agencies exclusively or semi-exclusively serve buyers within a vertical market. For instance, a marketing agency that only serves hotels would be considered a vertical specialist. Generalist agencies serve a broad range of businesses.

Access the Competitor Messaging in the companion workbook. At the top, you'll see two columns:

- Vertical Specialist
- Generalist

Under Vertical Specialist, add the name of your top three most significant vertical competitors. Under Generalist, write down your two most significant competitors that offer a similar service to yours but take a broad market approach.

Before proceeding to Step 2, share your list with your sales and client success leadership team to get their feedback and input.

STEP 2: RESEARCH YOUR COMPETITORS

Differentiation refers to the unique qualities, features, or advantages that a business uses to set itself or its products and services apart from its competitors.

We're going to look at four key components of differentiation that your competitors use on their websites. The good news is finding out how your competition differentiates their business isn't hard to do. Just visit two specific pages on their website: the homepage, and the services overview page(s).

The homepage is the most valuable piece of virtual real estate on an agency website. It gets the most traffic, and it also often creates the first impression that visitors form about the agency, its credibility, and its offerings. The homepage is where founders and their marketing teams spend most of their time and effort optimizing the copy.

The services overview page is where your competitor goes into greater detail about the features, attributes, and benefits of their services. This copy typically includes the problems they solve, unique selling points, social proof, and competitive advantages.

Deep Specialization Pro Tip: In terms of where to look for key messaging on these pages, the higher up on the page, the more important the message. Why? The limited real estate on a webpage, especially at its top, forces trade-offs. There is only one top of the page, so your competitors can't say everything about their service there. What they choose to put there is what they feel most aligns with their buyers (aka your buyers).

Document the four key components of competitive differentiation:

- Key Pains
- Key Benefits
- Positioning
- Proof Points

Here's a brief overview of each.

Key Pains

Key pains are the target buyer's problems and the consequential impacts of those problems. You could easily imagine a list of 20 to 30 pains that any good agency solves for a buyer, but we're not looking for a laundry list of pains. Instead, zero in on the prominent pains your competitors mention on their websites.

Here's a list of pains that an agency targeting law firms might have on its site:

- Not enough quality leads
- Losing high-value cases to your competition
- Not showing up on the first page of Google
- Ineffective marketing resulting in either no leads or, worse yet, wrong-fit clients
- A fragmented approach to marketing
- Time-consuming marketing
- Difficulty standing out in a crowded market

Deep Specialization Pro Tip: As you do this research, keep an eye out for a new pain you're not using or a better way to articulate your buyer's pains.

Key Benefits

Benefits are the positive results that your competitors use in their marketing materials. Similar to key pains, any agency can create a long list of the benefits of working with them, but because there is limited space on a website, they have to choose which benefits to highlight.

Note that *features* are the things a product does or its attributes. *Benefits* are the value and utility you get by having that feature. Here's an example using the iPhone.

Feature	Benefit
12 mega-pixel lens	Take sharper photos
20 hours of battery life	Charge your phone only once per day
Satellite connection for SOS calls	Peace of mind when you're off the grid

Positioning

Positioning is shaping the perception of where you stand in the market. Good positioning distinguishes you and establishes your uniqueness.

To use an example from the airline industry, let's compare Southwest Airlines with Delta Airlines.

	Southwest Airlines	Delta Airlines
Positioning	Low cost, no frills, a la carte	Premium, experience, all-inclusive

Both companies provide a similar service, but their positioning is quite different. Southwest Airlines appeals to value-conscious customers, while Delta Airlines attracts customers who are willing to pay more for a better overall flying experience.

Understanding how your competitors position themselves will help you find "white space" in the market to claim. Strategically, it's better to position your agency so that it is unique.

For example, if all the airlines are claiming to be low cost, no frills, and a la carte, and you're saying the same thing about your airline, it will be easy to ignore since it sounds like everyone else.

Companies, products, and services that are perceived as the same are considered commodities, and the only thing you can compete on when you're selling a commodity is price. When all else is equal, the cheaper solution wins. As an agency owner, you want to avoid being perceived as a commodity.

Here's a list of positioning-related messaging that an agency targeting law firms might have on its site:

- Everything your law firm needs when it comes to marketing. [All in one]
- Everything we do is customized to your needs—no cookie cutters here! [Customized]
- We are the largest provider. [Size advantage]
- We're lawyers too. [We won't try to sell you something you don't need]
- We walk our talk. [Integrity]
- Law firm websites for only $200 per month. [Low cost]
- The only SEO agency for lawyers with a 94% retention rate. [Our clients stay with us, and you will too]

We'll work on creating your unique positioning in Chapter 8, but for now, look at your competitors' positioning and document it in the Competitor Messaging template in the companion workbook.

Proof Points

Proof points are the hardworking data points that support and substantiate your marketing claims. Or as positioning expert April Dunford says, "The proof that you can deliver on the value you say you can."

Which claim is more credible?

Claim A
"We're the #1 home services marketing agency."

Claim B
"We're the #1 home services marketing agency.
81 of our plumbing clients doubled their revenue
in the last 12 months."

Claim B uses evidence, called a proof point, to back up its claim that it's the number one home services marketing agency.

Using proof points inspires confidence, establishes credibility, and helps overcome skepticism. Here are some more examples:

- If you make the claim that your reputation management service is the preferred choice by roofers, a proof point would be your five-star reviews by roofers.
- If you make the claim that your websites are designed by award-winning graphic designers, a proof point would be the number and types of design awards your designers have received.
- If you make the claim that your podcast agency gets more booked guests, a proof point would be sharing the number and types of guests you get for your clients on average.

Proof points turn marketing hype into believable statements of fact. Any agency can say whatever they want about how great its service is ("We're the best!"), but at the end of the day, how believable is it? Your claims become persuasive when you use objective, credible, and verifiable data to support them.

Knowing what proof points your competitors use will help you better understand the proof points that your vertical buyers care about. The research process can also uncover areas where you may have gaps in proof points that could make your agency more credible.

Proof points include:

- Awards (from a credible source)
- Client reviews and ratings
- Client success stories or case studies
- Data and statistics
- Expert endorsements

- Guarantees
- Press mentions
- Social media mentions
- Social proof
- Testimonials

Here are some more examples of agency-specific proof points:

- 32 five-star reviews on Google
- Our average client saves at least 15% in marketing costs in first 60 days
- Our "We've Got You Covered" guarantee protects you up to $1,000,000 in losses
- Average client onboards in less than ten days
- Inc. 5000 winner
- Average plumbing client grows by 41% annually

STEP 3: DOCUMENT YOUR FINDINGS

After you've added your five competitors' key pains, key benefits, positioning, and proof points to the Competitor Messaging worksheet, document your key takeaways, initial insights, and ideas for your own positioning.

For example, you may notice most of your competitors focus their positioning on results or low cost. Or maybe you're seeing an understanding of clients' marketing repeated as a key benefit.

In the next chapter, you'll combine what you've learned about your vertical buyer and your competitors with what makes you truly unique to create your vertical positioning.

CHAPTER TAKEAWAYS

- 90% of marketers see positive impacts from competitive research.
- Clients choose from a range of agency options, not just yours. Competitors are businesses that clients choose in your place or switch to after leaving you.
- Knowing your competitors helps you market and position your agency's brand.
- The most significant competitor might be a client's decision to maintain the status quo.

Step 3

Match Your Message to Your Vertical

DEEP SPECIALIZATION

Choose the Perfect
Vertical Market

Match Your Message
to Your Vertical

Build the Team

Study Your Vertical
Market Buyer

Plan Your
Campaigns

Chapter 8

Create Your Vertical Positioning

"In a busy marketplace, not standing out is the same as being invisible."

SETH GODIN, author of *Purple Cow*[39]

et's review where we're up to: You have chosen a vertical market and clarified what motivates clients to buy. You also have an understanding of who your competitors are and how they're distinguishing themselves. Now, let's talk about positioning your firm.

Positioning is the deliberate process of defining and establishing a distinctive place for your agency in the mind of the target client, relative to competing offerings. Your goal is to occupy a clear, unique, and advantageous position that makes your offering the most memorable and preferable.

It's important to remember that positioning is not about your product or service. It's about your buyer's perception. Al Ries and Jack Trout said it best in their seminal book *Positioning: The Battle for Your Mind*: "Positioning is not what you do to a product. Positioning is what you do to the mind of the prospect."[40]

VERTICAL POSITIONING PROCESS

☉ The vertical positioning process should take no more than two hours to get a working first draft. To assist you in this process, you can access the Vertical Positioning worksheet in the companion workbook.

There are four steps to create your vertical positioning:

- Step 1: Create a List of Attributes
- Step 2: Plot Your Attributes on an X-Y Axis
- Step 3: Choose Your Two Key Attributes
- Step 4: Create Your Vertical Positioning Statement

Step 1: Create a List of Attributes

Attributes are all the things your vertical client might want in an agency. You can also think of attributes as the features and capabilities of an ideal agency for your buyer.

These could include expertise in specific verticals or services, a strong track record of successful campaigns, effective communication, the ability to work within a budget, and innovative approaches. They define what makes an agency an ideal choice for a particular client's needs.

One of my clients is an agency that is an expert at providing long-term SEO strategies for their clients. Naturally, they tend to attract clients who value long-term SEO strategies over short-term SEO tactics. In this case, "long-term SEO strategies" would be an attribute of my client.

You can come up with your agency's attributes from your buyer journey client interviews and from your competitive analysis, plus your familiarity with your service offering and clients.

Here's a list of common agency attributes:

- All in one
- Community-focused
- Custom solutions
- Cutting-edge
- Done for you
- Original thinking
- Point solution
- Proactive support
- Results-focused
- Speed to results
- Thought leadership
- Transparency
- True partnership
- We care
- We specialize in a service

- We'll teach you how to become a marketer
- We're big
- We're small

If you need more inspiration, search "digital marketing agency" on Google, and browse through a handful of sites that come up.

Go ahead and make your list. You're looking for between 10 and 20 attributes for your agency.

Step 2: Plot Your Attributes on an X-Y Axis

Now pick any two attributes from the list you created, and plot them on a simple graph. It should look something like this:

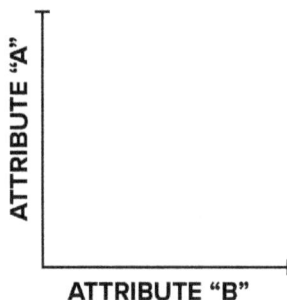

ATTRIBUTE "A" (vertical axis)

ATTRIBUTE "B" (horizontal axis)

To illustrate how this works, let's take the category of cars. Imagine for a moment that you're on the marketing team for Volvo. Out of all the attributes that a car buyer might want in a car, let's plot Brand Prestige and Performance in the chart.

We'll place Brand Prestige on the vertical axis (y), so

that the higher up you go on the chart, the more prestigious your car brand is considered.

Next, we'll put Performance on the horizontal axis (x), so that the farther to the right you go on this chart, the higher the performance of your cars.

Now, add your competitors' car brands into the graph, positioning them based on where they compete for Brand Prestige and Performance. Again, the more prestigious, the higher up they go on the chart. The higher the performance of their cars, the farther to the right they are. Use market research, competitor positioning (from Chapter 7), as well as your best judgment to guide you. Note: this is not an exact science.

Then place your own brand on the graph, which is Volvo in this example.

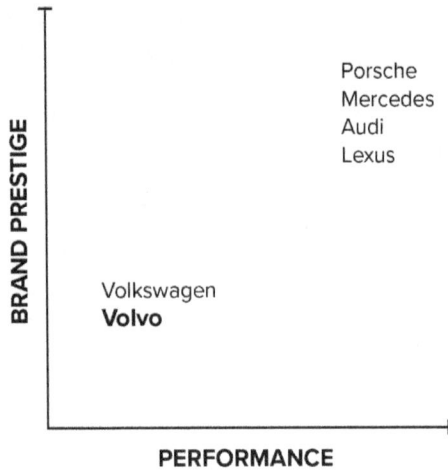

BRAND PRESTIGE (vertical axis)

Porsche
Mercedes
Audi
Lexus

Volkswagen
Volvo

PERFORMANCE

The graph reveals that Porsche, Mercedes, Audi, and Lexus are in the upper right corner, meaning they're already established as both prestigious and high-performance car brands.

Volvo and Volkswagen are in the lower left side of the chart because they are generally not regarded as either prestigious or high performance in the mind of the consumer.

The high-prestige and high-performance "upper right" segment of the car market is like a can of sardines. It's crowded and packed to the brim. It would not be wise for Volvo to even attempt to unseat these brands. That positioning has already been claimed, and there's not enough money in the world for Volvo to change that.

A better strategy is to use different attributes so they can find some "white space" in the market. They need to find a differentiated positioning that is unique to them.

Let's swap in the attributes Safety and Reliability, and place the same car brands in the graph.

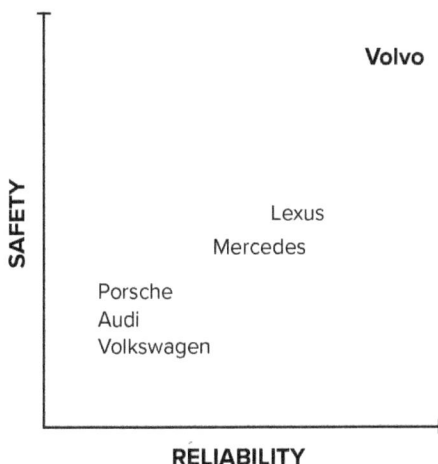

It turns out, with these two attributes, there is a lot of white space for Volvo.

Based on these two attributes, Volvo's positioning could be "We are the best-made, safest car on the road." And Volvo did just that[41] through a series of well-crafted advertisements over the years. These campaigns resulted in Volvo claiming the valuable position of the world's safest, most reliable car brand, while simultaneously differentiating from its competitors.

Step 3: Choose Your Two Key Attributes

Now it's your turn. Pull up your list of attributes, choose any two you like, and place them on the X and Y axes. Then position your brand, along with your competitors, in the graph accordingly. Keep doing this until you identify two attributes that place you in the "white space."

Step 4: Create Your Vertical Positioning Statement

Now with your two "white space" attributes, you can use this formula to create your vertical positioning statement: *We help [Vertical] with [Service] by blending [Attribute 1] and [Attribute 2].*

For example: *We help restoration companies with lead gen by blending speed-to-results and done-for-you marketing.*

What you end up with should be a clear and crisp positioning for your agency.

Don't overthink this process. Instead, approach it as creating a draft positioning statement, one that you will test, revisit, and refine over time.

Armed with your vertical positioning statement, next we'll focus on creating your agency's unique point of view.

| CHAPTER TAKEAWAYS

- Positioning helps differentiate your agency in the market and is based on buyers' perceptions.
- Choose attributes that allow you to occupy a unique position in the market ("white space").
- Your vertical positioning statement is a guide for your agency's messaging, not necessarily a tagline or copy to be used externally.
- Positioning is a continuous process of validation and refinement.

Chapter 9

Establish Your Point of View

> "People don't buy what you do,
> they buy why you do it."
>
> SIMON SINEK, author of *Start with Why*[42]

A point of view (POV) is a unique, differentiated perspective or stance that you have about a particular problem and your solution. Your POV is also like a moat around your agency: it's your durable competitive advantage.[43]

Here's the thing: agencies copy the best ideas from each other, whether it's attributes to attract clients or cost savings to build profits. They converge to similar services with similar cost structures. Due to the highly competitive agency marketplace, even within vertical markets, having differentiated positioning isn't enough. You need a strong POV.

Your POV isn't just about what you do; it's more about the change your agency brings to the vertical market you serve as a whole. Your POV articulates your vision for a new and improved future for your vertical that signals you genuinely care about them. If a vertical market is like a community, what are you doing as an agency to improve the community, not just some of the people in it?

Here's an example of a POV from Luke Eggebraaten, founder and CEO of Phaser Marketing, an agency targeting construction businesses.

> *The construction industry has a bad rap. We are losing all our boomers [in the industry] to retirement, and there's not a ton of people to replace them and yet construction is only going up.*
>
> *We exist to change that stigma. We want to help raise awareness about the merits of working in construction, so more people get into the trades.*[44]

○ To establish a baseline point of view for your agency, set aside about two hours. Start by accessing the Point of View worksheet in the companion workbook. There are four key steps to develop your POV:

- Identify the Big Problem We Solve
- Name the Villain
- A New Future
- A Bridge to the Future

IDENTIFY THE BIG PROBLEM WE SOLVE

Your agency creates value by solving a specific, functional problem. It could be helping clients generate good-fit leads, increase brand awareness, or improve conversion rates.

But we're not talking about solving those kinds of problems here. We're looking for an important, meaningful problem within the context of the vertical market you serve. It's a problem that is not being adequately addressed by existing solutions but that matters to your buyers. This problem is often a status quo problem facing your vertical market. Like quicksand, the status quo—the old way of doing things—is easy to get stuck in.

Here are a few examples of status quo problems:

- Small plumbing companies don't have the same access to effective and sophisticated marketing strategies as big plumbing companies.
- Lawyers aren't trained to be businesspeople.
- Only 3% of the internet is accessible to people with disabilities.
- People see trade careers as "dirty jobs" that are low paying and unprofessional.
- Manufacturing is shifting overseas, away from the USA.

Ask yourself: What is the status quo problem our vertical buyers care about? Write down the Big Problem We Solve in the Point of View worksheet.

Deep Specialization Pro Tip: Instead of promoting the benefits and features of your agency, evangelize the Big Problem We Solve to the vertical market community and your clients. The more clearly and accurately you articulate the big problem, the more people will naturally assume you know how to solve it.

NAME THE VILLAIN

The villain is a metaphorical enemy that represents the status quo problem your agency is solving. Having a clearly articulated villain is a way to rally clients and buyers in a vertical market around the problem by giving them something to stand against.

Your villain could be tools (e.g., disconnected systems), an outdated philosophy (e.g., diversity is irrelevant), another company (e.g., the big-name competitor), or the old way (e.g., interruption marketing).

For example, a brand that produces eco-friendly products might position plastic waste or pollution as the villain (an outdated philosophy). Other villains include:

- The negative stigma around careers in the trades
- On-premise software[45] (versus cloud-based software)
- Gas-powered cars
- Factory farming

Through its Real Beauty campaign, Dove positioned unrealistic beauty standards and the media's portrayal of women as the villain. Their message was about promoting real, natural beauty. As a result of this campaign, the company increased revenues by 10% in a single year.[46]

Here are a couple of tips for identifying your agency's villain:

- Choose a villain that your vertical buyer will immediately recognize. If it's not obvious, they won't get it.
- If your villain doesn't create an emotional reaction in your vertical buyer, it's likely too vague or off the mark.
- Choose a villain that you authentically care about defeating, but avoid resorting to unfounded negative portrayals.

Write down the villain in the Point of View worksheet.

A NEW FUTURE

The next aspect of your POV is articulating a new and different future where the villain has been defeated (thanks, in part, to your help).

- Is your villain the negative stigma around careers in the trades? Your new future may be a world where careers in the trades are revered and respected by all.
- Is your villain on-premise software? Your new future

may be a world where businesses of all shapes and sizes can affordably and easily access software in the cloud.

- Is your villain unrealistic beauty standards? Your new future may be a world where real, natural beauty is cherished.

You get the point. What will the world be like once you help defeat the villain? Write down your New Future in the Point of View worksheet.

A BRIDGE TO THE FUTURE

Now it's time to tie your agency to the New Future. This bridge needs to go beyond the functional work that you do for your clients and tap into your why. This is not a why about you, your family, or your wealth; instead, you need to communicate how your business is a part of the solution to the Big Problem and how you're helping to defeat the villain.

For example, by improving manufacturing companies' marketing, you're helping them to keep high-value projects in the U.S.

How does your agency serve as a Bridge to the New Future? Write down your Bridge to the New Future in the Point of View worksheet.

CREATE YOUR POV

Now that you've defined the big problem, named the villain, created a new future, and the bridge to the future, it's time to create your POV. There are three steps to creating a POV.[47]

Step 1: Frame the Problem and Name the Villain
Name the big problem you're intent on solving. For example, "There is a negative stigma around careers in the trades, which has led to a shortage of skilled workers."

Step 2: Evangelize a Different Future
Paint a picture of a time in the future when the big problem has been solved or has changed. This is the promise land that you're helping to create. For example, "We believe that careers in the trades should be seen as a viable and respectable career path that leads to significant job satisfaction and personal financial abundance."

Step 3: Show How Your Solution Bridges the Gap from the Problem to a Different Future
Show how your agency helps your vertical market transform by solving the problem and getting them closer to the new future. For example, "We work with our contractor clients to promote job openings at their companies, and we also position careers in the trades as a great option. We raise awareness by speaking at trade shows and working directly with local schools, and we have our

own scholarship for high school seniors going into the trades."

Let's bring it all together. Here's a POV statement from Luke Eggebraaten, founder and CEO of Phaser Marketing:

> *The negative stigma around careers in the trades has led to a shortage of skilled workers.*
>
> *At Phaser Marketing, we're different than other marketing agencies because we're committed to changing that. Our mission is to elevate the trades.*
>
> *We believe that careers in the trades should be seen as a viable and respectable career path that leads to significant job satisfaction and personal financial abundance.*
>
> *We work with our contractor clients to promote job openings at their companies, and we also help with positioning careers in the trades as a great option for young men and women.*
>
> *We evangelize the virtues of working in the trades by speaking at trade shows and working directly with local schools, and we have our own scholarship for high school seniors going into the trades.*
>
> *With Phaser Marketing, you're not just working with an agency; you're partnering with passionate advocates for the trades.*

Notice that this POV tells a very different story than what you typically see from agencies. Most agencies compete on easy-to-ignore, overused platitudes like "We try harder" or "We're an extension of your team." This POV puts Phaser Marketing in a different category.

Next up, I'll show you how to develop a handy guide for all your vertical messaging to live.

Tips for Creating Your POV

- Your POV should clearly show why and how your solution is different from (and preferably superior to) other existing solutions.
- A great POV connects emotionally with your target audience. It should resonate with a particular pain point or aspiration they have.
- You must passionately believe in and advocate for your POV, acting as an evangelist to spread the message and get others on board.

CHAPTER TAKEAWAYS

- A POV provides a unique stance on a status quo problem within your vertical market and offers a solution.
- A POV acts as a differentiator and competitive advantage for your agency.
- Your POV is not just about your services; it's about the larger change your agency brings to your vertical market.

Chapter 10

Develop Your Vertical Messaging Guide

"People don't buy the best products; they buy
the products they can understand the fastest."

DONALD MILLER, author of *Building a StoryBrand*[48]

Your Vertical Messaging Guide is an essential
document that allows you and your teams to incorporate high-quality vertical-specific messaging
in your marketing with consistency. A kind of North Star,
this guide serves as your agency's single source of truth
for all things vertical messaging.

The good news is it uses a lot of the material you've already collected so far. The seven sections of your Vertical
Messaging Guide are:

1. What Is Our Point of View?

2. What Is Our Vertical Positioning?
3. What Are the Attributes Our Vertical Buyers Care About?
4. What Are the Business Challenges We Solve?
5. What Are Our Clients' Intrinsic and Extrinsic Wins?
6. What Is the Transformation We Help Create?
7. What Are Our Proof Points?

⏱ Your Vertical Messaging Guide should take no more than four hours to complete. Follow the Vertical Messaging Guide worksheet, which you can find in the companion workbook.

Let's walk through each section in order. Since you've already prepared a bunch of this material, it's a matter of bringing it all together.

1. WHAT IS OUR POINT OF VIEW?

This is your point of view statement that you completed in the previous chapter.

Where and how to use your point of view: Once established, it's crucial that all messaging, branding, and communication related to your agency consistently reflect the POV.

2. WHAT IS OUR VERTICAL POSITIONING?

This is your vertical positioning statement that we completed in Chapter 8: *We help [Vertical] with [Service] by blending [Attribute 1] and [Attribute 2].*

Where and how to use your vertical positioning statement: Your vertical positioning statement can be used verbatim in marketing materials, and you can also use it as a guide for crafting various types of messaging (e.g., website copy, about us copy, etc.).

3. WHAT ARE THE ATTRIBUTES OUR VERTICAL BUYERS CARE ABOUT?

These are the attributes you found in Chapter 6. With your list in hand, mark each one of your attributes, features, or capabilities as either being unique or shared with other businesses you compete with. Knowing about and promoting your unique attributes is important as it enables differentiation, helps your agency stand out, and gives you a competitive advantage in the market.

Where and how to use your attributes: Share your unique attributes across your sales and marketing materials. Get the word out that what you have to offer is valuable to your vertical buyers!

4. WHAT ARE THE BUSINESS CHALLENGES WE SOLVE?

Unlike the big problem covered in the previous chapter on creating your POV, business challenges are the urgent and important problems that prevent vertical buyers from achieving their outcomes. They hire you to solve these problems.

You should have collected a list of challenges from your vertical clients in your one-on-one interviews (Chapter 6). You can also source challenges (or pains) from the competitor differentiation research you did in Chapter 7.

Make a list of the top five to ten business challenges your clients had before hiring your agency. To help you come up with ideas, here are some categories of business challenges and common pain points.

Marketing
- Ineffective strategies
- Attracting the wrong clients
- Negative reviews

People
- Inability to recruit and hire top players
- Staff turnover
- Poor morale

Productivity
- Too much wasted time

- Lacking automation
- Systems don't talk to each other

Process
- Inconsistent implementation
- Slow delivery times
- Lack of proven systems

Here are three business challenges that an agency client of mine solves:

- Ineffective marketing resulting in either zero leads or, worse yet, wrong-fit clients.
- Poor intake, causing loss of potential clients, damage to the firm's reputation, and decreased profitability.
- Staff turnover and inability to recruit A players, resulting in poor client experience and satisfaction.

Add the business challenges you solve to your Vertical Messaging Guide.

Where and how to use the business challenges: Add them to your marketing and sales materials to communicate the specific problems you solve for your vertical clients.

5. WHAT ARE OUR CLIENTS' INTRINSIC AND EXTRINSIC WINS?

These are the gains your clients get when you successfully solve the problem they hired you to solve. Intrinsic wins are their internal or emotional wins, whereas extrinsic wins are the external or tangible wins.

Make two lists: one of your clients' intrinsic wins and one of their extrinsic wins.

To help in building your lists, here's a list of common wins for agency clients:

Intrinsic wins
- Personal growth
- Overcome fears
- Improved confidence
- Reduced stress
- More creativity
- Greater job satisfaction
- Greater sense of freedom and independence
- Improved social status

Extrinsic wins
- More free time
- Gain new skills
- More money/raise/bonus
- Promotions
- Win awards
- Public recognition

- Earn certifications
- More social media likes and followers
- Better reviews and ratings
- Increased sales and profits
- New partnerships or endorsements

Here's an example of an intrinsic win for an agency client: *Lawyers who work with us build a life that they're proud of.*

Here's an example of an extrinsic win for an agency client: *Lawyers who work with us accelerate growth and are put on track to double their revenues, profit, and freedom in 12 months.*

You'll gather a sense of your vertical market's wins from client interviews and competitor research. Once you've finished drafting your clients' intrinsic and extrinsic wins, add them to your Vertical Messaging Guide.

Where and how to use intrinsic and extrinsic wins: These are not necessarily used verbatim in marketing materials but function as a guide for crafting messaging. They're usually internal, for your team.

6. WHAT IS THE TRANSFORMATION WE HELP CREATE?

Next, you want to document the transformation your clients go through by working with you. We'll use the from/to format, which is a powerful way to clearly depict the progress a client has made. Here's how you can frame transformations:

1. **Identify the Starting Point (*from*)**
   - Understand the initial challenges, problems, or situations the client faced.
   - Recognize their initial mindset, beliefs, skills, or circumstances.

2. **Identify the Ending Point (*to*)**
   - Define their desired outcomes, goals, or achievements.
   - Recognize the new mindset, beliefs, skills, or circumstances the client has achieved or is working towards.

3. **Formulate the Transformation (*from/to*)**
   - Use clear, concise language to connect the starting point with the ending point.
   - Ensure the transformation showcases a distinct change or improvement.

Here are some examples of agency-specific from/to transformations:
- We help attorneys go from a lawyer to a law firm owner.
- We take attorneys from having very little business IQ to feeling confident in their abilities to grow their law firms.

- We take clients from struggling with a stagnant sales growth of 2% annually to achieving a consistent 15% growth rate.

Deep Specialization Pro Tip: It's important that the change is genuine and based on actual results or progress. Overstating or fabricating results can damage your trust and credibility in a vertical market.

Once you've finished drafting these transformations, add them to your Vertical Messaging Guide.

Where and how to use the transformations: Use them across your sales and marketing materials.

7. WHAT ARE OUR PROOF POINTS?

As mentioned in Chapter 7, proof points are the evidence or data that support and substantiate your marketing claims. Claiming your agency is the best in the world is one thing, but providing credible data that supports this claim makes it real and effective.

Sharing vertical specific third-party proof points in your marketing dramatically improves trust with your vertical buyer. For example, if you're an agency targeting franchise businesses, being endorsed by the International Franchise Association would go a long way to establishing credibility.

Once you've finished drafting your proof points, add them to your Vertical Messaging Guide.

Where and how to use proof points: Because they're so great at making your messages more real and compelling, use proof points everywhere you talk about your service (website, content, advertising, social media, etc.).

Now you're ready to take the work you've done in the Vertical Messaging Guide and apply it to your marketing strategy, which we'll cover in the next step, Plan Your Campaigns.

| CHAPTER TAKEAWAYS

- The Vertical Messaging Guide serves as a centralized document that will ensure consistent and high-quality messaging for vertical marketing efforts.
- While some elements of the guide are used directly in marketing, others serve as internal references for crafting effective messaging.
- Remember to always use the guide as a foundation for all vertical-specific messaging and marketing initiatives.

A GENTLE REMINDER FOR
THE AMBITIOUS READER

I know you love marketing, but make sure you've worked through the previous chapters in order before you dive into planning your campaigns. You'll thank me later. ;)

Step 4

Plan Your Campaigns

DEEP SPECIALIZATION

Choose the Perfect Vertical Market ✓ — Study Your Vertical Market Buyer ✓ — Match Your Message to Your Vertical ✓ — ④ Plan Your Campaigns — ⑤ Build the Team

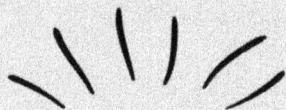

Hey, Corey here.

I hope you're enjoying the book so far, finding it both useful and practical. I have a favor to ask you. Would you please take a brief moment right now and leave an honest review of this book on Amazon?

Reviews are super important: they help other readers find the book and decide if it is right for them.

Thanks in advance,

AnyoneNotEveryone.com/review

Chapter 11

Vertical Sales and Marketing Strategies

"The essence of strategy is
choosing what not to do."

MICHAEL PORTER, creator of Porter's Five Forces framework[49]

C ongratulations! You've made it through the critical steps that so many others skip over.

Let's review where we're at: You've chosen a target vertical, researched your buyers and competitors, and developed your differentiated positioning and point of view. Now you're armed with everything you need to deploy marketing strategies that connect deeply with your vertical buyer and communicate that you are a deep specialist in their world.

There are three categories of sales and marketing activities for generating new clients in any vertical market:

- Inbound marketing
- Outbound sales and marketing
- Relationship marketing

I'll give you a brief overview of each, but first let's review the first two stages of the active buying process.

6 STAGES OF THE ACTIVE BUYING PROCESS

Need Recognition

↓

Information Gathering

↓

Evaluation

↓

Proposal

↓

Negotiation

↓

Purchase

Need Recognition happens when your vertical buyer has decided to make a change and starts seriously shopping around for an alternative agency. This typically happens when the company realizes the pain of continuing to do the same thing is greater than the pain of making a change. Less frequently, this can be initiated by a well-executed outbound campaign (more on this in Chapter 14).

Information Gathering, as the name suggests, is when

your vertical buyer is educating themselves on the options available to solve their marketing problem; they'll build a list of agencies for further evaluation.

Putting your brand, message, and offer in front of your vertical buyer during these two stages gives you an opportunity to be found, shape your buyers' perceptions, and influence who they partner with.

Your vertical buyers will only seriously shop a small handful of agencies—three to five at most. If you're not one of the agencies on the short list, the chances of your vertical buyer hiring you is pretty much zero.

Let's talk about the three types of marketing and how they can help you get on the short list.

INBOUND MARKETING

A useful definition for inbound marketing is putting your brand, message, and offer in front of your vertical buyers when they're in the *early stages* of the active buying process.

Building a business on inbounds alone is great in concept, but in practice, most agencies struggle with generating inbound leads consistently. That's in part because a very small fraction of your vertical market is in the active buying process at any one time.

Research from the B2B Institute at LinkedIn shows that as little as 5% of your target market are actively buying in a quarter.[50] Let's say that your vertical's total addressable market (TAM) is 1,000 businesses. At any one point, only 5% of them, or 50 buyers, are actively in the market.

Let's just say for argument's sake that there are 20 companies that are competitive with yours. Logically, that means you'll close 2.5 of the active buyers as new clients ($50 \div 20 = 2.5$).

But that's not the way it works. What actually happens is that one agency in your category is the dominant player, also known as the category king or queen, and they will get a disproportionate number of new clients—up to 76% of the new business.[51]

What this means for you, assuming you're not the category king or queen, is that you have to fight over the remaining 24% of the buyers looking for an agency.

Here's what the math looks like:

- Total addressable market: 1,000
- Number in active buying process: 50 (5% of TAM)
- Portion that go to the category kings or queens: 38 (up to 76% of TAM)
- Remaining clients for 19 agencies (including yours) to win: 12 (24% of TAM)
- New clients your agency wins: 1 or 2 (at best)

Looking at it from this perspective, unless you're already the category king or queen, inbounds will contribute to your growth, but it'll be slow going.

OUTBOUND SALES AND MARKETING

If a vertical buyer reaches out to you in the active buying process, they're likely in the information gathering stage and already considering other agencies.

If you want to skip the headache of RFPs (Request for Proposal), pitching, and dog-and-pony shows, you need to make sure your vertical buyers know your agency and what makes you different before they start shopping. This is where outbound sales and marketing come into play.

Outbound sales and marketing is the most powerful yet least understood and most underused client acquisition category used by agencies today.

Most people associate outbound sales with cold calls, rapid rejection, and pathetic performance. That's because, for most, it is.

The good news is you can generate plenty of new clients out of the other 95% of the target market—the ones who are not actively buying.

When you combine outbound sales and marketing with some of the principles I'm going to share with you in Chapter 14, you'll see surprising results.

Deep Specialization Pro Tip: Most agencies take a shotgun approach to outbound sales and marketing, hoping to hit something. Effective outbound requires more of a sniper approach.

RELATIONSHIP MARKETING

"Relationship" can sound like an odd word to use in the context of marketing. But **relationship marketing is the strategic cultivation of genuine person-to-person connections with influential individuals and natural social networks in your vertical market.** Most vertical market buyers discover their next agency via their social network. Therefore, your aim in marketing is to raise awareness, trust, and credibility of your agency within their social networks.

Author and consultant Philip Morgan says, "The ideas we are familiar with—digital marketing, content marketing, and so forth—become methods by which we can pursue the #1 goal of network expansion and enrichment. They are not, and never were, strategic goals or standalone systems that completely address our needs."[52] In other words, your inbound and outbound sales and marketing strategies are simply ways to connect with and build relationships with your buyers.

However, you don't need to rely solely on inbound and outbound sales and marketing strategies to generate new clients in your vertical market. You can deploy strategic relationship-building campaigns that accelerate awareness, trust, and credibility of your agency. We'll cover these in depth in Chapter 15.

In the next chapter, we'll zero in on the vertical-specific sales and marketing materials you need to be successful.

CHAPTER TAKEAWAYS

- The buying process has six stages, with the first two—Need Recognition and Information Gathering—being crucial for agencies to focus on.
- Agencies need to be one of the three to five options considered by buyers to have a real chance at being hired.
- While fruitful in theory, many agencies struggle to generate consistent inbound leads.
- Outbound marketing is a powerful strategy that's often underused or misunderstood. Beyond cold calls, it taps into the larger market not actively buying. Precision, not breadth, is key for effectiveness.
- Most agency hires come through personal recommendations or networks; relationships matter.

Chapter 12

Vertical Sales and Marketing Materials

"It's not what you sell that matters as much as how you sell it!"

BRIAN HALLIGAN, CEO and cofounder, HubSpot[53]

Research from Gartner says that about 57% of the purchasing decision is already made before a buyer contacts you to start the sales process.[54] That means that your vertical buyer will visit your website, check out your social media profiles, read online reviews, and visit other online sources before reaching out to you. What are they looking for?

They're assessing whether you understand them and the unique problem they're looking to solve, as well as if you can reliably solve it for them.

Therefore, the job of your sales and marketing assets is to convey those very things:

- You're a specialist in their vertical.
- You're intimately familiar with their problems.
- You can solve their problems.
- You've done it for others like them (and have evidence to prove it).

Here are the four vertical sales and marketing assets you'll need to get started:

1. Vertical Webpage
2. Vertical Client Success Stories
3. Vertical Client Testimonials
4. Vertical Social Proof

The good news is you've already created a lot of the building blocks you'll need for these assets in your Vertical Messaging Guide from Chapter 10. Let's go through each in turn.

From time to time, as I review the material in this section with my clients, they'll make a comment along the lines of "This feels like Marketing 101 stuff." They're making the point that what we're covering seems obvious. They're right. You may also feel the same way.

But while many agency owners know what to do, and may even guide their clients accordingly, they consistently neglect their own marketing efforts. They fail to prioritize their own marketing.

So, even if it seems basic, remember its significance. If you focus on just these four points, it'll set you on the right path.

CHECKLIST

To help with this process, use the Vertical Sales and Marketing Materials Checklist found in the companion workbook.

1. VERTICAL WEBPAGE

You need only one webpage dedicated to your vertical on your agency website. Over time, you can evolve your existing site or launch an entirely new site for your vertical buyer.

The job of this page is to communicate that you are a deep specialist in their vertical market. You can accomplish that by following these best practices.

Headline Copy

Your website headline, typically the large bold text at the top of your webpage, is a great place for your vertical positioning statement that we worked on back in Chapter 8. As a refresher, we used the formula: *We help [Vertical] with [Service] by blending [Attribute 1] and [Attribute 2].* For example:

We help personal injury attorneys with accelerating their law firm growth by blending done-for-you marketing with business coaching.

Using this positioning statement in your website headline gives your visitor a front-and-center understanding that you're a specialist in their vertical and that you're different from alternatives.

Sub-headline Copy

Your website sub-headline, typically the smaller copy just below your headline, is a great place to include some or all of your point of view (found in your Vertical Messaging Guide). Putting your POV in your sub-headline quickly conveys empathy for your vertical buyer. For example:

Lawyers aren't trained to be business owners. Let's change that.

Body Copy

Across the body of your webpage, typically the sections below the sub-headline, you'll want to use your vertical market's insider language. We introduced the concept of insider language back in Chapter 2. In short, every vertical market has terms and phrases that you'll want to master and convey in your copy to communicate that you're an insider in their world.

For example, if you're helping lawyers with lead gen, you would use the word "cases," not "jobs," "business," or "patients." If you're working with plumbers, you'd use "jobs."

But don't just use insider language. Create content that is useful and engaging. Author Ann Handley says it well: "Quality content means content that is packed with clear utility and is brimming with inspiration, and ... has relentless empathy for the audience."[55]

Images

Use images of people in your vertical on your webpage. For example, if your vertical is attorneys, include images of real attorneys throughout your site. Akin to seeing a familiar face in a crowd, using images of your vertical clients signals to website visitors that you're a specialist in their vertical market.

Deep Specialization Pro Tip: Schedule a photo shoot at a vertical client's workplace. You'll get genuine and credible photos for your website and marketing materials.

Other Things to Add to Your Vertical Webpage

- Your attributes (from the Vertical Messaging Guide)
- The business challenges you solve (from the Vertical Messaging Guide)
- Your proof points (from the Vertical Messaging Guide)
- Vertical client success stories (more below)

- Vertical client testimonials (more below)

2. VERTICAL CLIENT SUCCESS STORIES

Client success stories are also called case studies. I personally dislike the term "case study" because it conjures up images of long-winded clinical reports filled with walls of text. Plus, it's more powerful to use a story framework when sharing your clients' successes.

Use this effective framework to craft a persuasive client success story:

- **Before:** The emotional and rational challenges your client was struggling with before they hired you to fix their problem.
- **During:** What you did to help them fix their problem once they hired you.
- **After:** The emotional and rational impact on your client's business and life after they started with you.

Notice that I included both the emotional and rational impacts. This is intentional, because it's easy to overlook the emotional impact in the realm of business and clients. Interestingly, your buyers will connect with the emotional language at a deeper level.

Here's an example of a client success story that uses this framework.

Before

"I Don't Trust Any of These Marketing Companies"

By the time Tim Flynn encountered Scorpion, he had already been put through the wringer by marketing companies who had sold him a bill of goods but seemed to care more about taking his hard-earned money than delivering real results. He made no secret of his distrust (and even disdain) for digital marketing as a whole.

Tim was so passionate about solving this problem that he created a presentation that detailed exactly how he wanted his marketing strategy to go—because he felt this was necessary to protect his business. His only remaining task was to find a partner who would actually deliver.

During

From Overwhelming Waste to Real Results

Tim's detailed presentation showed just how passionate he is about his company's success and future. We took this to heart, taking the time to understand exactly what he wanted. We worked with him to create a plan of action that would make this a reality. We identified who we would target, where we would target, and why, and we built a detailed strategy to show exactly how we would spend his hard-earned marketing dollars.

After

A Partnership Turned Friendship

Since partnering with Scorpion in 2016, Tim has been able to expand his business significantly, setting new records for revenue in 2019 and planning for two new locations in 2020.

Here are some of the results Tim experienced:

- 2,470% increase in organic web traffic
- 30% increase in advertising leads
- 35% increase in total leads

We're proud to build lasting friendships with great home services business owners like Tim Flynn. We love you, Tim![56]

Best Practices for Client Success Stories
- Create success stories about vertical clients who are like the types of clients you want to attract. For example, if you want clients with ten or more employees, create client success stories about clients with ten or more employees.
- Tell the story using both emotion and data. A client success story with all emotion and no data is not very convincing. A client success story with all data and no emotion isn't persuasive. Instead, use both.
- Include real names, actual client images, and/or

videos. This helps bring the story to life and improves its believability.

Quick brainstorm: Make a list of clients whom you want to ask for a client success story. Feel free to use the companion workbook or a simple pencil and paper.

3. VERTICAL CLIENT TESTIMONIALS

Testimonials serve as powerful endorsements of the results your agency can achieve. A statement about your agency's performance is always more impactful when it comes from a satisfied client rather than from you.

Don't just collect testimonials from vertical clients. Make them more impactful by using these two formats: outcome-focused testimonials and transformational testimonials.

Outcome-Focused Testimonials

These testimonials help you communicate the outcomes your agency provides with more persuasion and credibility.

Follow these steps to create outcome-focused testimonials:

1. **Identify Desired Outcomes:** List three to five key results that clients in your vertical are seeking, and which your agency can deliver.

2. **Use Previous Insights:** To determine what your target clients really want, refer to the buyer journey client interviews and Vertical Messaging Guide discussed in Chapters 6 and 10.

3. **Request Specific Testimonials:** Approach your clients and ask them to provide testimonials, highlighting how they achieved the desired outcomes through your agency.

For instance, if your clients want clear marketing performance reports, a powerful testimonial might be: "Before switching to Acme Agency, we'd spend over two hours each week trying to understand our reports. Now, we invest just 15 minutes and have a clear grasp on our marketing campaigns."

4. **Aim for Diversity:** Try to gather at least one testimonial for each of the key outcomes you've identified.

Deep Specialization Pro Tip: This method is also a great way to tackle sales objections. By understanding common objections, you can gather client testimonials that address and neutralize these concerns for prospective clients.

Transformational Testimonials

Transformational testimonials are compelling narratives that showcase your agency's ability to catalyze change, turning challenges into successes. They underscore your agency's impact, painting a vivid before-and-after picture.

In Chapter 10, we delved into the concept of client transformations and saw the power of from/to stories. Now let's translate that understanding into impactful testimonials using the from/to approach. Here are some examples of from/to testimonials:

"We went from having boring, ineffective training that nobody liked to a fully trained team bursting with confidence."

"We went from having upset clients to clients who finally trusted us again."

"I transformed from being overwhelmed by chaos to navigating with clear direction and confidence."

Remember, **potential clients are not just buying your service; they're investing in the transformation you promise.** Highlighting these transformations using client testimonials in your marketing amplifies your agency's value proposition.

Quick brainstorm: Make a list of clients whom you want to ask for a testimonial. Feel free to use the companion workbook or a simple pencil and paper.

4. VERTICAL SOCIAL PROOF

Simply put, social proof is when we look to others to determine what is correct or acceptable. If a lot of people in your vertical are endorsing your agency, others are more likely to hire you.

In addition to client success stories and testimonials, you'll want to collect vertical-specific reviews and ratings as well as awards and endorsements.

Reviews and Ratings

Enhance your reputation by collecting ratings and reviews from vertical clients on well-known review platforms such as Google, Yelp, and Clutch.co. Check if there are reputable directories and review sites specific to your vertical. If they exist, ensure your agency is listed and actively gather reviews from vertical clients there.

Then incorporate these ratings and reviews into your marketing materials for added credibility. It's effective: **88% of consumers trust online reviews as much as personal recommendations.**[57]

Quick brainstorm: Go to the companion workbook and fill in your current ratings.

Awards and Endorsements

In addition to general industry accolades like the Webby Awards, aim for awards specific to your vertical market. For instance, the digital marketing firm Scorpion—where I was chief marketing officer for nearly seven years—was recognized as the number one franchise marketing company by *Entrepreneur* magazine two years in a row.[58] Winning this award not once but twice reinforced our credibility and improved our visibility in the franchise vertical.

In addition to specific awards, seek endorsements from reputable companies and influential figures in your vertical. To find trustworthy endorsers:

- Identify industry leaders, including relevant industry associations and organizations; industry-focused media like magazines, blogs, or newspapers; and experts and thought leaders known for their significant contributions to the vertical.
- Tap into your existing network, especially those in your vertical.

Remember, it's crucial that endorsements are authentic and based on genuine respect. Endorsements should vouch for your agency's abilities, not just be a formality or transaction. When coupled with testimonials that come from your clients, endorsements from influential figures in your vertical make a compelling case to your potential clients.

Quick brainstorm: Make a list of vertical awards and endorsements you want to pursue. Feel free to use the companion workbook or a simple pencil and paper.

Next up, we're going to do a deep dive into vertical-specific inbound marketing strategies.

| CHAPTER TAKEAWAYS

- About 57% of a purchasing decision is made before a buyer contacts you, meaning they've already checked your website, social media, reviews, etc.
- Potential clients assess whether you understand their unique problem and if you can reliably solve it for them.
- Your key messages—communicated through your webpage, client success stories, testimonials, and social proof—should demonstrate your ability to solve these problems and provide evidence of past success with similar clients.

Chapter 13

Vertical Inbound Marketing Strategies

> "Best way to sell something: don't sell anything. Earn the awareness, respect, and trust of those who might buy."
>
> RAND FISHKIN, cofounder of Moz[59]

The primary aim of inbound marketing is to position your agency so that when your vertical buyer is actively seeking solutions, your agency's brand emerges with the right message and offer.

My definition of inbound marketing includes everything from paid ads to content marketing, SEO, social media content, and email marketing. Since you're an agency owner, I presume you're already familiar with the basic approaches for these tactics. Therefore, this chapter will zoom in on specific tactics that have been especially effective for vertically specialized agencies, based on my experience and insights from those I've collaborated with or featured on my *Deep Specialization* podcast.

I'll focus on three types of vertical-specific inbound tactics:

- Thought Leadership and Content Marketing
- Speak at and/or Host Events
- Paid Advertising

CHECKLIST

You can access a comprehensive Vertical Inbound Marketing checklist in the companion workbook.

THOUGHT LEADERSHIP AND CONTENT MARKETING

Regardless of the medium (e.g., video, written copy, audio) or format (e.g., blog, newsletter, webinar, speech, podcast), your aim is to create helpful content that answers questions that your vertical is asking, either explicitly or implicitly.

Marketing expert Ann Handley writes, "Ridiculously good content is content that your audience values in one way or another."[60] Remember, you possess expertise in both your agency's digital marketing services and this specific vertical market. You are uniquely positioned to create content that provides significant value to them, be it through solving problems, offering insights, or simply entertaining them.

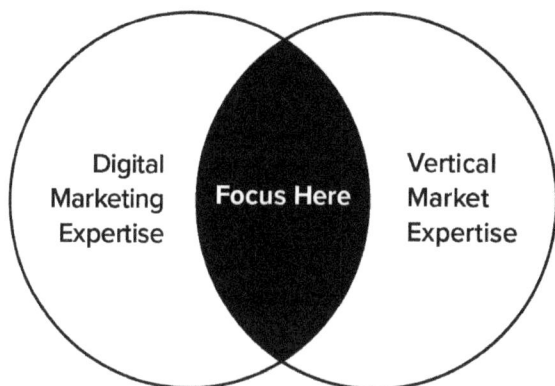

"We're putting out a lot of content just around problems and solving those problems and those questions that attorneys are asking. Attorneys who have a problem, they say, 'Hey, these guys are pretty credible.'"

CHASE WILLIAMS, founder and managing partner at Market My Market[61]

Channels where you can distribute your helpful, vertical-specific content include:

- LinkedIn posts (organic)
- Webinars
- Books—physical, audio, or digital
- Newsletter
- YouTube video
- Your website (for SEO)
- Podcast (more below)
- Podcast tour (more below)
- Speaking at events (more below)

The channels you choose to focus your thought leadership content on will depend on your preferences. Do you like being on video? Then YouTube might be right for you. Do you like writing? Then a newsletter and articles could be the way to go.

Xaña Winans built up her seven-figure agency focused on dentists, Golden Proportions, by providing written thought leadership to the dental industry. This includes a dedicated column in *Dentistry Today* on marketing for dentists.[62]

Launch a Podcast

As of this writing, launching a podcast is one of my favorite ways to build awareness for an agency within a vertical market.[63] It's a relatively quick way to build credibility and brand awareness of your agency, not to mention the following benefits.

Lead Generation

Over time, your vertical market podcast can become your biggest source for new leads. Chris Yano, founder of RYNO Strategic Services, an agency targeting HVAC businesses, launched his show, *To the Point—Home Services Podcast,*[64] a few years back and today gets 50,000 downloads per month. The podcast has become their main source of new leads. Chris recently shared this with me about his massively successful podcast:

> *You start to build trust just because [target clients] are listening to you. I might share something that someone listening hears and says, "Yep, I gotta make sure I implement that."*
>
> *Also, I'm bringing on some of my biggest clients, having them share all the things that I know the listener is going to run into—that builds a trust, right?*
>
> *The volume [of] people that reach out from that podcast that want do business with RYNO is exponential. And so, it works. It's become our largest lead source.*[65]

Network with Influential People

Interviewing highly regarded vertical market authors, thought leaders, and influencers on your podcast gives you backdoor access to otherwise hard-to-reach people. By inviting them on your podcast, you're giving them a platform to share their story and grow their following. You're also spending valuable time with them, laying the foundation for a personal connection.

Hosting an interview-style podcast is a great way to learn about your vertical buyers and the industry as a whole.

Getting Started

Today, it's easier than ever to launch a podcast. Two options are to do it yourself (with internal resources) or to work with a podcast production company. Of these two, my recommendation is to hire a podcast production company to take care of the details, so you can focus on the strategy and content.

A good podcast production company will typically guide you in setting the overall strategy, finding and securing guests, editing the episodes, creating show notes and social clips, publishing the episodes, and more.

Deep Specialization Pro Tip: Find a podcast production company that has at least two years' experience working with business-to-business (B2B) clients. Bonus if they work with other digital agencies.

Podcast Tour

Podcast tours are popular in the book industry, where authors guest on popular podcasts in a short time to promote their latest work. For your agency, think of it as a tailored strategy: guesting on niche podcasts that cater to your vertical market. By discussing topics and solutions that showcase your expertise tailored to the vertical, you can:

- Increase visibility in your vertical market
- Establish yourself as an authority
- Strengthen relationships with potential clients and partners in the vertical

Getting on these podcasts is a matter of building a list of vertical podcasts and prioritizing them based on relevance (does the podcast cater directly to your vertical market?) and reach (what's the podcast's listenership size?). You can use tools like Rephonic to help you find the podcasts for your list.

Once you have a prioritized list, you'll want to reach out with a personalized email. In the email, express genuine interest in their podcast and explain how your discussion can benefit their audience. Keep in mind, podcast hosts are looking for ways to reach new listeners, so let them know that you'll help promote the episode to your audience.

You can get a detailed 16-minute video walkthrough of this process along with outreach scripts in the online workbook (available at AnyoneNotEveryone.com).

SPEAK AT EVENTS

Speaking at vertical events and conferences will help you build your reputation as an expert. Event organizers prefer speakers who add value to their event, resonate with the intended audience, and create a memorable experience. Here are ways to increase your chances of being selected to speak:

- Organizers want speakers who are experts in their field. Showcase your achievements, credentials, case studies, and areas of specialization.
- Align your content with the event's objectives, audience, and theme. Understand the purpose of the event and pitch topics that resonate with that.
- Organizers look for fresh and innovative ideas. Offer a unique perspective or groundbreaking insights.
- Having a track record of speaking at similar events or conferences is a huge plus. Send them your speaker portfolio with videos or reviews of past presentations.

Keep in mind, being asked to speak on the main stage requires a great deal of trust and credibility that builds over time. As you're getting there, take other speaking opportunities available to you, such as speaking on a panel or hosting a breakout. All are valuable. As agency positioning expert David C. Baker says, "One keynote is worth three breakouts, and one breakout is worth four thousand appearances on a panel."[66]

HOST EVENTS

Hosting an event for your vertical market, whether in person or virtually, can create deeper connections and often results in new leads. Here are some examples of agencies running this play successfully.

Virtual Events

SMB Team, an agency targeting attorneys, hosts a virtual three-day event every quarter. The content is centered on providing high-value advice and business frameworks to attorneys who want to accelerate their growth. What started off as a webinar series grew to a Tony Robbins–style three days of marketing coaching and mindset transformation that's attended by thousands of attorneys every quarter. Today, it generates $3 million in new business every quarter and is the primary source of new business for the $40 million agency.[67]

When I asked SMB Team's CEO, Bill Hauser, about the impact his events have on his agency, he told me, "I think the events have the biggest impact from the goodwill that they create; it's significant to give someone that much value in a world where everyone's asking for something."[68]

In-Person Events

Scorpion, an agency specializing in legal, home services, and other verticals, organized a series of in-person events named the Home Services Road Show in various

American cities. These events were primarily attended by founders of small to mid-sized HVAC businesses. Instead of having a formal agenda or meeting in a lackluster conference room, we held them in private rooms at upscale steak houses, giving HVAC entrepreneurs a relaxed environment to network over delicious meals and cocktails. Although these events required significant planning, they ultimately yielded a positive return on investment.

RYNO Strategic Solutions hosts an invite-only, multi-day high-ticket annual event for home services called RYNOx.[69] They bring in A-list speakers and entertainers such as Gary Vaynerchuk, Mike Tyson, and Nelly, as well as business leaders from within the HVAC industry. It's a hot-ticket event that everyone in the industry wants to get in on.

PAID ADVERTISING

In addition to running paid ads on Google, LinkedIn, YouTube, and Facebook, there are a few other places to consider allocating your paid advertising dollars to directly reach your vertical buyers.

Sponsor Vertical Podcasts

If there are podcasts that are popular with your vertical market, you should consider advertising on a few episodes.

This will help put your brand, message, and offer in front of their audience, which of course is the same people you're targeting.

For example, if you're targeting chain restaurants, you might consider sponsoring a popular podcast targeting leaders in the restaurant industry, such as *Restaurant Unstoppable*.[70]

You can find popular podcasts in your vertical market by doing a few Google searches (e.g., "best [vertical] podcasts") or by using a tool like Rephonic.

Sponsor Vertical Associations and Publications

Vertical associations, such as the National Restaurant Association,[71] and publications, such as *QSR* magazine,[72] often offer a variety of opportunities to advertise on their media properties. This includes everything from sponsoring their email newsletter to placing banner ads on their website to paying them to publish your content in their media. We'll revisit the topic of leveraging vertical associations and publications to grow your agency in Chapter 15.

INBOUNDS AREN'T ENOUGH

While inbound marketing is an important channel, agencies shouldn't rely on inbound alone if they want to scale revenue. My friend and customer development consultant Rory Clark recently said to me: "The problem with inbound is that you get what comes, right? If you like donuts and all that's coming in is cookies, that's not good."[73]

In the next chapter, we're going to cover vertical outbound sales and marketing strategies. In it, you'll learn how to use tools like gift marketing to get the best clients available in your vertical market.

CHAPTER TAKEAWAYS

- Amplify your inbound marketing efforts with vertical-specific content marketing, podcasts, events, sponsorships, and more.
- Create content that blends your expertise in digital marketing and in the vertical by answering questions specific to your market.
- Podcasts are an effective way to quickly establish credibility and raise your profile in a vertical.
- Being a guest on niche podcasts increases visibility, establishes authority, and strengthens relationships in the vertical.
- Virtual and in-person events provide an opportunity to provide high-value content and build trust with your buyers in your vertical.

Chapter 14

Vertical Outbound Sales and Marketing Strategies

"The best way to predict the
future is to create it."

PETER DRUCKER, father of modern management theory[74]

R emember what customer development consultant
Rory Clark said about the limits of inbound marketing? Here he is again on the benefits of outbound
marketing: "When you go outbound, if you say you like
donuts, you go out and look for donuts. That's the benefit
of outbounding. You can go get the exact customers you
want instead of taking what's coming to you."[75]

Vertical outbound sales and marketing simply means
reaching out to your buyers proactively, rather than waiting for them to come to you. As mentioned in Chapter
11, only 5% of your vertical market is actively buying each

quarter. So, not only are you competing for this small percentage of active buyers, but 95% of your target market isn't even searching for a new agency.

Let's take a closer look at the 95% through a concept called the Zone of Indifference.[76]

Take a normal distribution curve to represent your vertical market. The line measures your vertical buyers' level of happiness with their current agency. We'll call this the Happiness Curve.

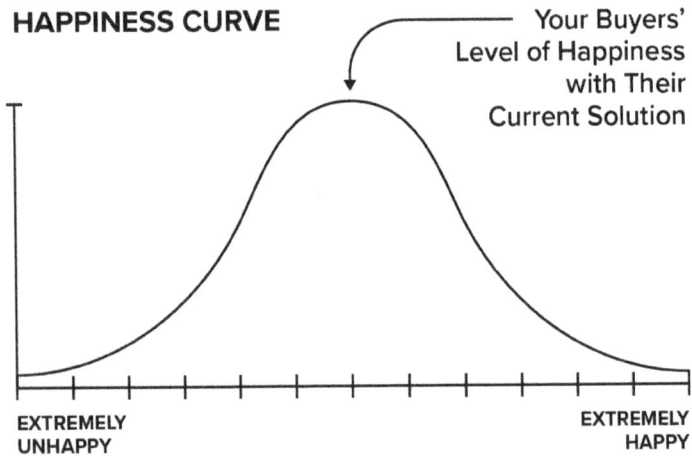

HAPPINESS CURVE

Your Buyers'
Level of Happiness
with Their
Current Solution

EXTREMELY
UNHAPPY

EXTREMELY
HAPPY

On the far right end of the Happiness Curve, you have a relatively small number of clients who are extremely happy and satisfied with their current agency. According to a study by Lee Research, only 8% of clients said they were strongly satisfied with their experience.[77] Hopefully, that 8% includes some of your agency's clients!

HAPPINESS CURVE

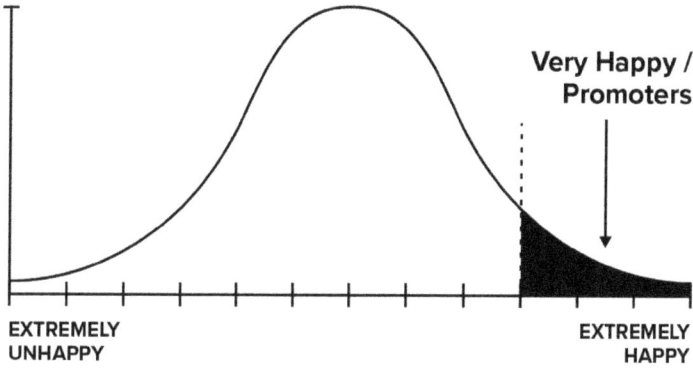

Very Happy / Promoters

EXTREMELY
UNHAPPY

EXTREMELY
HAPPY

They're on the extremely happy end of the Happiness Curve. These people actively recommend their current agency to others and voluntarily evangelize the brand among friends and colleagues. It's unlikely they'll switch from their agency anytime soon because they are so happy.

HAPPINESS CURVE

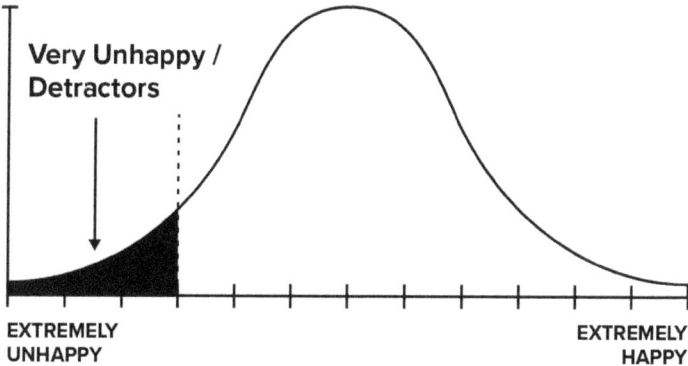

Very Unhappy / Detractors

EXTREMELY
UNHAPPY

EXTREMELY
HAPPY

On the left end of the Happiness Curve are the folks who are very unhappy with their current agency. These are the roughly 5% clients who have decided to find a new agency and are in the active buying process, as described in Chapter 11. If you have a well-executed vertical inbound marketing strategy in place (discussed in Chapter 13), you'll capture a share of these leads.

What you have in the middle of the Happiness Curve is called the Zone of Indifference, and that's where *most* of your vertical buyers are right now—upwards of 80% of your total addressable market (TAM).

HAPPINESS CURVE

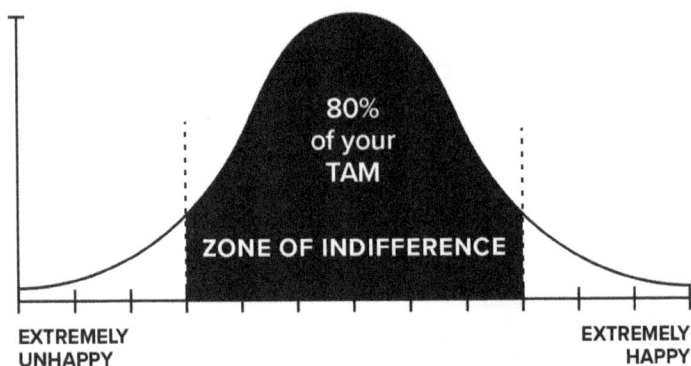

Here's a quick story to help illustrate what the Zone of Indifference is all about.

My wife has an iPhone 11. As of this writing, the latest model is the iPhone 15, making her phone four years old. Her iPhone behaves like the weather in a mountain town: erratic and unreliable. Her phone is slow, the apps crash from time to time, her photo storage is maxed out, and it has a short battery life. She complains about it ... quite a lot.

When I ask her why she doesn't just go out to the Verizon store and upgrade to the latest iPhone, she says, "I'll get to it."

But she never does.

When it comes to my wife's iPhone, she's in the Zone of Indifference.

She's stuck in between extremely happy and extremely unhappy. The perceived pain of upgrading to the new phone is greater than the perceived benefits she would get with the new phone, so she puts it off for now.

According to research from Wilson Learning,[78] agency clients in the Zone of Indifference:

- Tend not to express their dissatisfaction, meaning there is no opportunity for recovery
- Are relatively easy for a competitor to steal away
- Are not a positive source of referrals

To put it simply, instead of just waiting for very dissatisfied customers to find you, if you want more control over your business growth, you need to prospect into the Zone of Indifference. This large zone is exactly where your competitor agencies are at risk of losing their clients.

"Bottom line, if 80% of customers are neither loyal nor dissatisfied, there is a greater risk of customer defection from the largest segment of your customer population."

Wilson Learning Website[79]

If that's true, why then do traditional outbound techniques fail so frequently?

For example, a study by the Keller Research Center at Baylor University found that after 6,264 cold calls were placed over a seven-day period, agents were able to set a total of 19 appointments with prospective clients, equaling a 0.3% success rate.[80]

COMMON MISTAKES AGENCIES MAKE GOING OUTBOUND

Agencies make two major mistakes, contributing to their outbound struggles.

Poor Targeting

Poor targeting comes from insufficient research into the vertical market's preferences and needs. A spam-your-TAM approach leads to a vacuum of true empathy and a heavy reliance on lead list quantity over quality. When you depend on shady third-party prospect lists, you get unreliable and unqualified leads who don't respond or frequently flake out on their appointments.

Easy-to-Ignore Creative

When your vertical buyer sees your email come through her inbox, it looks and feels the same as the ten other ones she got today. Like a whisper in a storm, typical outbound messages are ignored because they lack uniqueness, are too generic, and are sometimes overly clever at the cost of being clear. As author Donald Miller astutely says, "If you confuse, you lose."[81]

FOUR SECRETS TO UNLOCK OUTBOUND FOR YOUR AGENCY

Here's how to create a consistently positive return on your outbound:

1. Develop expertise in a specific vertical market
2. Build a 20% lead list
3. Send a gift that is unique, striking, and leaves an impression
4. Be persistent, yet patient

1. Develop Expertise in a Specific Vertical Market

Has this ever happened to you?

You're at a party struggling to make small talk with some random partygoer you've just met. You're standing there, with a clear plastic cup in one hand and a cocktail napkin in the other, trying to look interested in what they're saying. Yet inside, you're dying. You think, "I've gotta get outta here."

Then, all of a sudden, they say something that clicks.

Their mom used to be your fourth-grade teacher. Or they were in the same fraternity or sorority as you. Or they lived in the same apartment building as you did in your twenties. Or you both love the same brand of chips. It could be anything that connects you.

Now that you're connected, it changes the whole dynamic of the conversation. That shared history moves them from a stranger to a friend. The energy between the two of you goes from resistance to comfort and flow. It's like adding motor oil to a jammed-up engine: having a shared experience or interest makes everything operate better.

This is like what happens when you are a true expert in the same vertical market as your prospect. You're able to move from resistance to trust much faster because you're relatable to them.

For example, attorneys in private practice today probably get ten emails and five calls a day from agencies eager to help with their marketing. (It's a popular target market.) Most of the outbound copy is sloppy, spray-and-pray attempts at getting the attorney's attention.

Those messages are ignored.

But the carefully crafted messages that truly zero in on the unique world of an attorney who is trying to grow their practice get through. They get noticed because they communicate that the sender (you) understands the attorney's world. That's thanks to Deep Specialization: you can solve unique problems for attorneys.

Bottom line: specializing in a vertical market improves the likelihood your outbound messages will be noticed. But I hope by this point in the book you already know this.

2. Build a 20% Lead List

Let's be honest, list building isn't very sexy. In fact, it's quite boring.

But in my opinion, agency owners don't obsess over creating a high-quality lead list for going outbound. Instead, they prefer to do the minimum so that they can jump right into messaging, email sequencing, and other flashier parts of the outbound process.

But **using a low-quality lead list is like a house built on sand: it's likely to fail.** That's because everything downstream from the lead list (email subject lines, landing pages, offers, closes, etc.) depends on getting to the right person.

List building done right improves the likelihood your target prospects will be interested, resulting in better engagement, more appointments, and faster sales growth. As Joey Gilkey, CEO of Apex Revenue, says, "The list is the strategy."[82]

My number one rule for outbound list building is **Quality Beats Quantity.**

Apply the Pareto principle (the 80/20 rule) to your list, and build a 20% lead list. In other words, prioritize the businesses that have the potential of being the best fit in your vertical market.

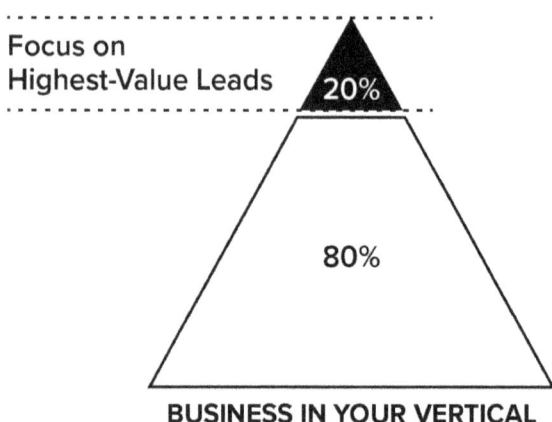

Focus on Highest-Value Leads

20%

80%

BUSINESS IN YOUR VERTICAL

Here are the two steps for creating a 20% lead list for outbound.

Step 1: Source the Leads

There are four main ways to find leads for your outbound campaigns.

Create a List Yourself

Build your list of vertical market businesses by scraping publicly available data via online directories such as Google Business Profile or vertical-specific directories.[83] There are several web-scraping tools available online to help with this. If you're not particularly techy, or just prefer to outsource it, find a freelancer online who specializes in data scraping on sites like Fiverr or Upwork.

Find a Trusted Partner Willing to Share Their Lead List with You

This trusted partner could be a referral partner or an indirect competitor who targets the same vertical market as you. For example, let's say you're a digital marketing agency building a lead list of dentists. You could reach out to your referral partner—a SaaS business also targeting dentists—to see if they'll share their list with you, or even do a list swap with you.

Buy a List from a Research Firm

In some vertical markets and industries, there are research firms specialized in that industry that offer lead lists for sale. These lists tend to be expensive, but the quality is typically very high. For example, you can buy a database of restaurant leaders from Technomic, a research and consulting firm specializing in the restaurant industry.[84]

Buy a List from a Broker Service

The fourth option is to purchase a list directly from a broker such as ZoomInfo, Dun and Bradstreet, or similar list brokerages.

These four options are listed in order of the amount of control you have over who gets on your target lead list. When you create the list yourself, you have complete control of who makes it onto your lead list. But when you buy a list from a broker, you're purchasing a large bucket of faceless leads—you have no idea where they came from (they won't tell you), whether the data is good, or if the leads are actually in your target market.

My strong recommendation is to build your own list. Doing so ensures you have a high-quality list that you can rely on throughout the prospecting process.

Deep Specialization Pro Tip: Regardless of the source of the leads, build and maintain an internal database of all the businesses in your vertical. Yes, I know it's a lot of work, but you're building a house on a rock-solid foundation!

Step 2: Prioritize the List

Once you have a high-quality list of leads in your vertical market, the next thing to do is prioritize the list. You want to isolate the top 20% of the businesses with the highest value to your agency.

Prioritize by Need

Let's say your agency sells websites to dentists. Go to Wayback Machine[85] and look up each of the dentists on your target lead list to see when they last had a website redesign. A dentist's website generally has a life span of three years. If a dentist's website is three years old or older, as verified on the Wayback Machine archive, it's likely they need a new one. These dentists should be prioritized on your list over those who have recently updated their websites, say, two months ago.

Prioritize by Ability to Afford

Continuing with the dentist example, when targeting dentists for your website design services, prioritize practices with multiple dentists or multiple locations. The logic is that these practices are likely to have a larger website budget compared to solo practices in one location.

Once you have prioritized your list by need and ability to afford, only go outbound to those top businesses and forget the rest.

Again, you may think these steps are a lot of trouble for a lead list. And you're right: it is a lot of work. Here's the thing: the work of sorting through leads will either happen at the front end of the campaign or the back end. The work itself is inevitable, and if you push it to the back end, you'll end up sending a lot of questionable leads to your sales team. Wouldn't you rather they spend time on highly qualified and motivated target clients?

Plus, doing this now will be worth it because once you

have your 20% lead list, the next step is to send them an eye-opening gift in the mail.

3. Send a Gift That Is Unique, Striking, and Leaves an Impression

For many, going outbound means peppering your target leads with a persistent sequence of cold emails, cold calls, and cold LinkedIn InMails. It's the default process agencies and third-party lead gen companies take.

Whether your target audience is attorneys, B2B manufacturing companies, or schools, they're receiving five to ten cold outreaches per day from firms just like yours. To your vertical leads, they are a nuisance and are often simply ignored.

Why?

Because there isn't an existing relationship between you and the target lead. There's no familiarity, no history, and no trust to build off at all. But what if you could transform your cold outreach into a warm outreach? This is where gifts come in. Here's a quick story.

At Scorpion, over a period of a few years, we sent thousands of personal injury attorneys a Scorpion-branded tin of amazingly delicious cookies. We had never spoken with these attorneys, but we sent them cookies. Why?

First, we had a high-quality list that we built, which was prioritized by need and ability to afford. Only the best personal injury attorney leads got the cookies.

Second, we had attempted cold-calling them for months but achieved minimal success because the attorneys' gatekeepers often blocked our efforts. The gatekeepers for personal injury attorneys are the receptionists and office managers who answer incoming calls and screen out random people soliciting their business. It's their job to prevent the salesperson at Scorpion or any other agency from ever reaching the attorney who, in our case, was the decision-maker we needed to speak with.

So, instead of persisting with cold calls to little return, we sent the attorney a gift: an overnight delivery of delicious cookies. The delivery would bypass the mailroom and instead arrive on the attorney's desk. Upon opening the delivery and discovering the cookies, they'd end up sharing them with the staff. What happened next was pure magic. The attorney or office staff would inevitably ask "Who sent these amazing cookies?" creating a stir in the office where everyone was talking about this company Scorpion that sent these delicious morsels of delight.

Not surprisingly, the next time the Scorpion salesperson called into the attorney's office, they'd experience a completely different tone from the gatekeeper. It went from "Sorry, the attorney isn't available" to "Oh, you're from Scorpion?! Thank you so much for those amazing cookies! The attorney would like to speak with you. Please hold." And then we'd be put through.

Why did sending a gift like a $50 tin of delicious cookies transform the dynamic between the Scorpion salesperson, the attorney, and their gatekeeper?

Because the attorney's experience of receiving the cookies was *unique* (no one else sent him amazing cookies), *striking* (it interrupted his day in a delightful way), and it left an *impression* (it got him and his staff curious about this strange company called Scorpion).

The impact of this gift was so significant in reversing the typical sales resistance and increasing outbound appointments that it set a new standard for all our outbound campaigns.

The new standard is called a **Uniquely Striking Impression,**[86] or USI.

Here's what it means: every gift you send to your 20% lead list needs to be unique, striking, and leave an impression. The power of USI gifts goes beyond just sending cookies.

Over the years, I've sent the following gifts as a first-touch sales outreach:

- Cookies to attorneys
- Donuts and coffee to plumbers
- Flowers to dentists
- Alcohol to attorneys
- iPads to franchise brand CMOs
- Books to plumbers
- Video brochures to everyone

What USI Gift Is Right for Your Vertical Buyer?

Sending cookies has worked across industries—who doesn't like delicious cookies? But you can also change up your USI to pair well with your vertical.

For example, don't send plumbers flowers because it wouldn't create the right impression (and it would probably have the undesired effect of communicating that you don't understand them very well). Instead, deliver glazed donuts and coffee to them.

Bottom line: don't take a one-size-fits-all approach to choosing your USI gift for your vertical. Instead, use these criteria to generate ideas that would work for your Deep Specialization:

- Is it unique? (Don't just send them a cheap pen with your logo on it.)
- Is it striking? (It should interrupt their day in a positive way.)
- Does it leave the right impression? (What you send should communicate that you understand them and value them as a potential future client.)

Leaving the right impression also avoids communicating that the gift is a quid pro quo, or a conditional relationship. Instead, you want to communicate generosity and genuine interest in building a real relationship. The author of *Giftology*, John Ruhlin, said it well: "It's the thoughtful thought that counts."[87]

If your USI idea meets all three of these criteria, it's likely you have a gift that will transform your outreach from cold to warm.

Deep Specialization Pro Tip: In our post-COVID world, not everyone goes to the office. To ensure your USI gift arrives at the right location, call the main office line ahead of sending the gift. Tell them you're sending your buyer a gift and ask them where you should send it. They won't likely give you the home address, but they can forward it on your behalf.

4. Be Persistent, Yet Patient

Outbound sales and marketing aren't hard. Sticking with it is.

One of the things that helps to maintain consistency with outbound campaigns is knowing the life cycle of the product or service you sell.

For example, Americans buy a new home every nine years on average. Americans buy a new car every five years on average. Dentists get a new website every three years on average.

That means that every dentist over a three-year period will likely be in the market for a new website. Sure, this could mean they stay with their current provider, but they may also shop other providers.

This is important because if you're persistent with sending USI gifts to your high-quality dentist leads over a long enough period of time, you'll be top of mind when they're ready for a new website. Why? Because at some point during that three-year period, they will have realized they needed a new website.

I recommend sending your high-quality leads a USI gift once every quarter. Each gift needs to be followed up with a coordinated sales outreach.

Continue to do this quarterly gift and sales outreach program until your leads tell you they chose to go with someone else or they agreed to meet with you.

Combining Sales Outreach with Your USI Gifts

For the best results, pair each USI gift with a proactive sales outreach. Even if the USI gift leaves a strong impression, most prospects won't initiate contact. It's crucial to reach out to them while you're on their mind.

Your seller's follow-up on USI gifts should be timely, consistent, and personalized.

The outreach should be the day of or no later than the day after they receive the USI gift. If the seller can't immediately engage with the buyer, they should continue outreach efforts with additional emails and calls over the next two to three weeks for a minimum of seven attempts.

For the best results, avoid blasting out generically written emails. Instead, have your sellers take the time to craft personalized emails and use call scripts that aren't completely canned. Also send articles, podcast episodes, or videos that actually help. Doing so will reinforce the message you're sending with the USI gift: you're genuinely interested in connecting with them specifically.

You should expect 3% to 5% of your targets to respond or engage. Focus on those new opportunities, and start planning your next USI gift. The targets who don't respond will still receive the USI gift, giving your sellers a valuable, high-quality touchpoint, the impact of which will compound over time.

In the next chapter, we're going to dive deep into vertical-specific relationship marketing strategies.

| CHAPTER TAKEAWAYS

- If you want control over your growth, you need to proactively reach out to potential clients rather than waiting for them to initiate contact.
- Target the Zone of Indifference: 80% of your vertical market is indifferent to their current agency, but they are not actively looking for a new agency.
- Agencies fail at outbound due to poor targeting and unremarkable creative messaging.
- Resist the urge to buy a lead list; build your own.
- A well-executed USI gift campaign—that is unique, striking, and leaves an impression— yields a response or engagement rate of 3% to 5%, with the impact of these touchpoints compounding over time.

Chapter 15

Vertical Relationship Sales and Marketing Strategies

"When people are overwhelmed with information and develop immunity to traditional forms of communication, they turn instead for advice and information to the people in their lives whom they respect, admire, and trust."

MALCOLM GLADWELL, author of The Tipping Point[88]

According to a *Harvard Business Review* article,[89] 80% to 90% of buyers have a set of vendors in mind before they do any research, and 90% of them will ultimately choose a vendor from their "day one" list. The article goes on to say there are three routes to get on the day one list:

- Colleague recommendations
- Previous experience with a vendor
- Vendor websites

In this chapter, you'll learn how to get on the day one list by becoming the go-to agency that gets recommended by colleagues from within your vertical market.

It Takes Time to Build Your Reputation

The communities within vertical markets are like villages, complete with preexisting networks built upon years of trust-building. When you commit to serving a vertical market, it's like moving into this village. Initially, your agency may be considered an outsider, but as time passes and your agency builds a reputation and trust, it becomes an integral part of the village community.

Attorney marketing agency BluShark Digital's founder Seth Price shared with me, "I look at the conference world like dating. You go to a vertical conference for the first time, a 'first date,' maybe you get a bite to eat, great. By the second time you go to the same conference, it's like seeing a friend. But the third one, you're now long-lost friends, like you're family."

Here are some strategies to effectively build trust in your vertical.

Prioritize the Tastemakers

Tastemakers are individuals or businesses that significantly influence which agencies are popularly accepted and used within a vertical market. Tastemakers come in two flavors: influential brands, and mavens.

Influential Brands

Within your vertical are just a few businesses that, if you're lucky enough to land as clients, will result in an immediate credibility boost and visibility for your agency within the vertical. I call these businesses influential brands.

At Scorpion, we were fortunate to have a senior executive on our team who had a preexisting relationship with a senior executive at the largest and most influential brand in the franchise industry.

This franchise brand was widely regarded as the most well-run organization in the industry. Their peers, whether they are large franchises or emerging franchises, look up to this industry leader for guidance and best practices.

The existing relationship with our executive led to this prominent franchise brand becoming one of our earliest major clients in the sector. This was a significant milestone, as we previously had no major clients in this sector, even though we saw great potential for our product and revenue growth there.

We saw this as our golden chance to boost Scorpion's visibility. We provided exceptional service to their account, even if it meant operating at a loss. If they were delighted with our work, it would significantly enhance our reputation and standing within the franchise community.

As a result of our success with this influential franchise brand, word-of-mouth referrals led to the rapid growth of our franchise vertical, making it our most significant vertical in terms of both client base and revenue within just a few years.

There are three steps to closing your first influential brand as a client.

Step 1: Identify Top Brands in Your Vertical Market

Do online research to identify the most successful brands in your vertical, since business success is highly correlated with influence. Look for indicators of their influence, such as:

- Business success and growth
- Involvement in vertical-specific associations
- Recognition from significant industry and business awards (e.g., Inc. 5000)

Step 2: Discover Existing Connections

Use existing relationships within your network or client list to identify mutual connections that could introduce you to the influential brands in your vertical market.

Investigate within your company to identify direct (first-degree) and indirect (second-degree) connections to individuals associated with the influential brands.

Step 3: Leverage Your Network to Connect with Key Decision-Makers

Establishing a connection with top executives at prominent brands can be challenging, especially with limited or weak ties. However, even a faint connection can be a starting point to stand out and build trust, personalize your approach, and offer genuine value. When researching the top executives, consider these questions to understand their needs and provide valuable insights:

- What goals are they pursuing?
- What projects are they working on?
- What currently holds significance for them?
- In what areas might they need assistance?

The answers to these questions will help ensure you lead with value.

Deep Specialization Pro Tip: Avoid generic or impersonal communication methods like sending case studies or irrelevant information. Focus on building relationships over making a quick sale.

Mavens

Mavens,[90] a term coined by Malcolm Gladwell in his book *The Tipping Point*, are catalysts for change who know an unusually high number of people within a vertical. They are the go-to individuals whenever one seeks knowledge on any subject, always in the loop and well-informed. They are like sheep herders in a world of herd mentality.

Mavens start "word-of-mouth epidemics" through their knowledge, social skills, and effective communication.

Most importantly, mavens are more likely to spread the news about your agency within your vertical and *be believed.*

Similar to influential brands, you'll want to put a concentrated focus on bringing mavens on your "team" through authentic relationship-building.

Who are they?

They could be successful business owners within the vertical, keynote speakers, notable authors, or editors of the vertical publications. Finding them is typically not that hard to do. Their names come up in client conversations, conferences, and online forums.

For example, one of my clients focuses on the restaurant industry. Within this vertical, there is a leading figure who is the editor of *QSR* magazine, a major industry publication. He publishes daily to his large following on LinkedIn, speaks at industry conferences, and is highly influential.

We identified him as a key influencer or maven. We made it a point to attend the same conferences he did, engage with his LinkedIn content, and consistently seek opportunities to connect with him. This built a genuine relationship between my client and this maven, leading to new business opportunities, a credible reference, and increased visibility for my client's brand in the restaurant sector.

Here are a few ways to work with the mavens within your vertical:

- **Talk with them frequently:** They typically have their finger on the pulse of the vertical, so having an open and regular dialogue with them means you'll stay top of mind and on top of vertical trends.
- **Invest in the relationship:** If you have the opportunity, take them out to dinner, go see a show, or do a fun activity together. Doing so creates shared memories and deepens the relationship.
- **Invite them to special events/announcements:** If your company has exclusive sneak peek content or other experiences reserved for VIPs, make sure you include your mavens.
- **Host their expenses at the industry conference:** This one works especially well for clients who are mavens. I've had great success sponsoring client mavens' conference tickets, flights, and hotels (first-class all the way). It also gives them a reason to talk about you and the experience you've created for them.

Vertical Associations

Regardless of the vertical you choose to focus on, there will always be at least one, but probably many more than one, professional or trade association within that vertical that is important for you to get involved with.

The benefits of getting involved include:

- **Fish in a Barrel:** Unlike general business events or conferences, vertical associations bring together stakeholders who have a direct interest in the vertical. Mavens, tastemakers, and opinion leaders are intimately connected with their associations.

- **Industry Insights:** Vertical associations often conduct research, studies, and surveys specific to their industry. Being part of the association gives you access to these insights, which can be invaluable when building or strengthening business relationships.
- **Credibility:** Getting involved with a recognized association signifies that you're serious about understanding and catering to the unique requirements and challenges of the vertical.

It can be tempting for agencies targeting a vertical to just run out and join an association without a plan. Doing so would be a mistake. Here's what to do instead.

Build a List of Vertical Associations

Ask your existing clients in your vertical about the associations they're affiliated with. Before joining an association you're interested in, check with your clients to see if they're members or if they recommend you join. Here are some examples of associations by vertical:

Healthcare:
- American Medical Association (AMA)
- American Hospital Association (AHA)
- American Dental Association (ADA)

Real Estate:

- National Association of Realtors (NAR)
- International Council of Shopping Centers (ICSC)

Hospitality

- American Hotel & Lodging Association (AHLA)
- National Restaurant Association

Retail

- National Retail Federation (NRF)
- Retail Industry Leaders Association (RILA)

You can also investigate which associations your competitors belong to. While their membership doesn't guarantee it's a suitable association for your agency, it's worth considering for your list.

Talk with the Associations

Get an understanding of the makeup of their membership to ensure it aligns with your vertical buyer. For example, if your primary target is senior executives from major restaurant chains, joining an association for bartenders might not be relevant.

Join and Get Involved

Once you've identified one or more associations you'd like to join, you need to take one last critical step: commit to getting involved. Simply paying the membership fee without engaging is a mistake I and many others have made.

Joining an association means more than paying the annual dues. That's like joining a health club and never going. You don't get results that way.

To truly harness the benefits of an association, active participation is key. Consider these options:

- Contribute to their publication or newsletter.
- Guest on their podcast.
- Provide content for their webinars.
- Speak at their events or set up a booth.
- Join their committees.
- Engage in their online communities.

Golden Proportion's founder, Xaña Winans, recently told me, "I recommend getting involved in consulting groups or business management groups that often are large and kind of support and serve an industry. Getting an affiliation with those larger groups or anybody that offers continuing education, and just being where they go to learn something new, that's where you want to be."[91]

The goal? Increase your visibility by providing value to the association's members. This will foster awareness and trust in your agency beyond what paid ads can achieve.

Remember, this is a marathon, not a sprint. Building trust and prominence in a vertical via an association requires commitment. It might take a couple of years, but the results—enhanced word-of-mouth, increased referrals, and smoother sales—can represent up to 80% of new business.

Vertical Conferences and Events

Attending vertical conferences and events allows you to connect with potential clients and strengthen bonds with existing ones. More than a chance for face-to-face interaction, these events offer the unique benefit of creating in-person shared experiences that simply cannot be replicated through Zoom, webinars, or emails.

Why are shared experiences vital?

Such moments foster deeper connections as they become lasting memories. As Joseph Pine II and James H. Gilmore aptly put it in *The Experience Economy*, **"If you didn't create a memory, it wasn't an economically distinctive experience."**[92]

However, a genuine shared experience goes beyond just inviting someone to your booth. Here's how to craft unforgettable moments at vertical conferences and events.

Host an Event

Organizing a successful event at a conference is about much more than securing a venue; it's about curating an experience. The scale can vary significantly—from grand soirees at upscale venues complete with entertainment, gourmet meals, and exquisite beverages to an intimate gathering at the conference hotel's bar where you can swipe your credit card.

Here are some tips for making a memorable event:

- **Understand Your Audience:** Know the preferences and interests of your guests. This will help you tailor the event to their liking, ensuring they feel considered and catered to.
- **Choose the Right Setting:** The venue sets the tone. Whether it's a lavish banquet hall or a cozy corner in a bar, ensure the environment promotes easy conversation and interaction.
- **Incorporate Entertainment:** Depending on your budget and the preferences of your guests, consider adding live music, a magician, or even a keynote speaker who can captivate your audience.
- **Serve Quality Food and Drinks:** Everyone appreciates good food and drink. Cater to diverse dietary needs and preferences, and if possible, choose dishes that are conversation starters.
- **Encourage Interaction:** Create opportunities for guests to mingle. This could be through organized activities, icebreaker games, or arranging the seating in a way that encourages conversation.
- **Personal Touches:** Personalizing the event—be it through customized name tags, thoughtful gifts, or even just personal greetings—can make your guests feel valued and appreciated.

The primary goal is to foster an atmosphere that allows you to forge meaningful connections with clients and prospects. It's those personal touches, combined with a well-planned event, that leaves a lasting impression.

Do a Unique Group Activity

Nothing creates memories faster than orchestrating a unique, fun, and enjoyable activity with your clients and prospects.

In addition to creating memories, unique group activities help to distinguish your brand from competitors, create a buzz (leading to word-of-mouth and social media sharing), as well as reflect the values, ethos, and culture of your company, giving prospects a clearer picture of who you are beyond the services you offer.

Here are some group activities I've either done as an agency CMO or other agency founders have done successfully:

- Front-row seats at a Britney Spears concert (or another headliner)
- Drive $250,000-plus exotic cars at a racetrack in Vegas
- Ride in a hot air balloon
- Host a round of golf with a $1,000,000 hole-in-one contest[93]
- Host a dinner at an exclusive restaurant
- Host a private meet-and-greet with a well-known author or celebrity

Conference Booths

Some agency founders I know love having a booth at a vertical conference, while others hate doing them. Here are some of the benefits of hosting a booth at a conference:

- **Convenience:** You're giving your clients and prospective clients an easy way to find you at the show.
- **Visibility:** A booth is a great way for new potential clients to discover you.
- **Relevance:** For major conferences, not having a booth can signal to your buyer that your business is no longer relevant (going out of business, refocusing away from the vertical, etc.). Hungry competitors at the show will take your absence as an opportunity to magnify this signal.

Here are some things to keep in mind if you're investing in a booth:

- **Be Remarkable:** Remember the USI standard we discussed in Chapter 14? Your booth should embody it. Aim for every aspect—from the theme to the giveaways to the swag items—to be unique, striking, and impactful. While you don't need to go as far as giving away a Tesla (like I did once), don't settle for the cheapest logoed pens either. Opt for high-quality booth swag that attendees will appreciate and use. Consider offering premium water bottles or upscale pens, even if in limited quantities. After all, isn't it better if people actually use and showcase your branded items? Prioritizing quality not only demonstrates your commitment to excellence and detail but also distances your brand from the negative perception of cheap products that end up in a landfill. High-quality swag stands a better chance of finding a place on someone's desk, reminding them of your brand's values.

- **The Conference Is Won before It Begins:** Hosting a booth requires a colossal amount of time. Between coordinating with vendors, shipping promotional items, and handling travel logistics, not to mention time spent away from the office and home, it's a substantial investment. Don't do all that work just to arrive at the booth for a few days expecting a steady flow of eager, highly qualified prospects to magically show up. Instead, **engineer your success at the conference before the conference begins**. Begin engaging with clients and potential leads long before the event.

Here are some strategies to prospect effectively before a conference:

- **Research the Attendees:** Look at the list of registered attendees, speakers, and participating companies if available. Identify key individuals and companies that you want to engage with.
- **Leverage Social Media:** Engage in conference-related

discussions on platforms like LinkedIn and X (formerly Twitter). Use the conference's official hashtag to increase visibility.

- **Send Personalized Invitations:** Reach out via email, inviting specific prospects to meet up during the conference. Look for opportunities to meet during slow times, such as breakfast, lunch, or just after sessions get out. Provide a clear value proposition that explains why they should visit your booth or schedule a meeting.
- **Leverage Existing Contacts:** Ask your current clients, partners, or other contacts if they'll be attending and if they can introduce you to any potential leads.

By being proactive and strategic in your approach, you can lay the groundwork for a successful conference, making sure you connect with the most valuable leads and make the most of the event.

Be Generous

Having a unique experience or giveaway at your booth is a great way to attract prospects. The key here is to offer something your vertical buyer would love to have, while at the same time is a bit of an indulgence. Some ideas include:

- Free headshots taken by a professional photographer
- Nordstrom shopping spree

- Luxury vacation giveaway
- Sports car giveaway[94]

Chase Williams, founder and managing partner at Market My Market, shared this cool booth lead generation idea with me:

> *We got the attendee list like two weeks before the conference, and I think there was like 800 or so people attending that we wanted to go after. So, we did an audit for every single one of them in two weeks. When someone walked by our booth, we'd say, "Hey, Corey from Quinn Law Firm, hang on a second, I have something for you." And they go, "What? What are you talking about?" We had a file folder with the audits printed out and said, "Oh, we made this for your firm." And they go, "What?" And I said, "Yeah, yeah, we did."*[95]

He went on to say it was a very successful tactic in creating conversations with their high-quality prospects at their booth.

Before we wrap up this section, it would be a missed opportunity if we didn't talk about speaking from the stage at vertical conferences and events. We covered it in Chapter 13, under Thought Leadership. Go check it out!

VERTICAL WATERING HOLES

In addition to vertical associations and conferences, find the "watering holes" where your vertical market buyers hang out. Common watering hole channels include:

- Facebook groups
- LinkedIn groups
- X/Twitter chats
- Instagram hashtags
- Pinterest boards
- YouTube channels
- Slack communities
- Reddit forums

Positioning expert Jonathan Stark advises an "answerbomb" strategy in watering holes:

Find places where the folks in your target market gather to talk shop. Search for emotionally charged language (e.g., love, hate, sucks, dream, nightmare, crazy) and requests for assistance (e.g., does anybody ..., help with ...). If you find someone who you can help, drop an "answerbomb" on them, in the form of a super detailed and actionable answer. If you blow their mind and they need more help, they'll be fairly likely to go to your profile and contact you directly.[96]

Next up, you'll learn the key roles for building vertical market expertise in the final step of Deep Specialization, Build Your Team.

CHAPTER TAKEAWAYS

- Prioritize building relationships with key vertical tastemakers such as influential brands and mavens to increase recommendations in your vertical market.
- Vertical associations bring together key stakeholders and influential figures in the market.
- Vertical conferences and events allow you to create in-person shared experiences, fostering deeper connections that cannot be replicated remotely.
- Genuine shared experiences go beyond mere interactions; they must be crafted in order to create lasting memories.

Step 5

Build the Team

DEEP SPECIALIZATION

Choose the Perfect
Vertical Market

Match Your Message
to Your Vertical

Build the Team

Study Your Vertical
Market Buyer

Plan Your
Campaigns

Chapter 16

Build the Team

"The bigger your goals become,
the better the Whos you'll need."

DAN SULLIVAN and DR. BENJAMIN HARDY,
authors of *Who Not How* [97]

O kay, let's review where we're at: you've chosen
a vertical market, researched both your buyers
and the competitors, developed your unique positioning and point of view, and you've considered which
types of marketing campaigns make the most sense for
your firm. Time for the final step: build the team.

Here's the good news. Getting early wins and building
momentum in your new vertical doesn't require you to
run out and hire new people. You can start where you are
and with the team you have.

Here's the (potentially) bad news. **The best person in**

your agency to own this strategy is you. I get it: your time is sucked dry, and you're focusing on a thousand different things to keep the ship afloat.

Here's something I already know about you. The fact that you've made it to this chapter tells me that you're serious about shifting away from serving clients of all shapes and sizes to focusing on a specific vertical market. You're ready to end the dependency on you, the founder, for sourcing and closing all the sales. You're ready to end the client churn. You're ready to end the unpredictable growth. You're ready to do what it takes to point your agency in a better direction.

So, remember our discussion on giving a damn, in Chapter 4? We emphasized how pivotal client intimacy is to succeeding in this strategy. It's not just about knowing your client's business but truly understanding their needs, challenges, aspirations, and the intricacies that make them unique. This depth of understanding forms the bedrock of our approach.

As the founder and leader of your agency, your role goes beyond business operations or strategy. You set the tone, the values, and the direction for your entire agency. Therefore, it is imperative that you, above all, genuinely understand and resonate with your vertical buyer.

Your intimate knowledge of them will not only guide your agency's strategies and decisions but also inspire your team to follow suit. The deeper your connection and understanding, the more tailored and effective your solutions will be, positioning your agency as the go-to expert in your vertical.

However, you are not the only person who is likely to be involved.

FUNCTIONAL SKILLS BY CHAPTER

Here's a chart outlining the required functional skills for each phase of this strategy. Depending on your situation, you might already have the functional expertise internally or you might need to outsource.

Chapter	Activity	Functional Skills
5. The Four-Step Process	Research existing clients and vertical markets	Strategy Market research
6. Get into the Mind of Your Vertical Buyer	Client interviews	Strategy Client communication
7. Know Your Vertical Competition	Research competitor messaging	Strategy Market research
8. Create Your Vertical Positioning	Develop differentiated positioning	Strategy
9. Establish Your Point of View	Develop your point of view	Strategy
10. Develop Your Vertical Messaging Guide	Create messaging guide	Strategy
12. Vertical Sales and Marketing Materials	Create marketing collateral	Strategy Copywriting Design Web development

13. Vertical Inbound Marketing Strategies	Create and execute vertical inbound campaigns	Inbound strategy Content strategy Copywriting Design Web developer Lead gen Sales
14. Vertical Outbound Sales and Marketing Strategies	Create and execute outbound campaigns	Outbound strategy Sales Copywriting Design Web developer Logistics
15. Vertical Relationship Sales and Marketing Strategies	Create and execute relationship campaigns	Relationship marketing strategy Sales Copywriting Design Web developer Logistics

SHOULD YOU USE INTERNAL OR EXTERNAL RESOURCES?

My rule of thumb is to use your internal resources first and contract second. Using internal resources allows you to tap into your existing processes and thereby move more quickly, and it's typically more cost-effective than outsourcing.

However, building true expertise in a vertical market takes time. You can expect a minimum of 18 to 24 months of continual focus on the vertical to build true expertise and brand awareness.

Most agency founders aren't going to accept an 18- to 24-month time period to build a deep understanding of a vertical. To expedite the process, there are two roles you could externally contract in the short term to save you 12 to 15 months.

Use These External Resources to Expedite Results

Vertical Subject Matter Experts

One of my consulting clients decided to focus his business on chain restaurants in the U.S. While he already had 22 chain restaurants as current clients, he was not an insider in the chain restaurant world at all. His background was in running sales teams for youth sports training programs. He didn't know who the key influencers were in the restaurant industry, the best conferences to attend, the right associations to get involved with, or the best content to create.

To bridge this knowledge gap, we hired a restaurant technology consultant, whom I discovered on LinkedIn while researching restaurant writers. This consultant had over two decades of experience in both executive roles at restaurant chains and in marketing for SaaS businesses targeting these chains.

Within weeks, she provided us with a comprehensive and prioritized list of industry-specific conferences, associations, influencers, editors, and podcasts. Beyond that, she connected us to prominent industry figures, introduced us to insider off-the-radar conferences, and linked us with CEOs of potential partner companies that had a vast clientele of chain restaurants.

> If you don't have existing insider knowledge or contacts within your vertical market, you can hire a vertical subject matter expert to help shorten your learning curve.

Here are some things to look for when hiring a vertical subject matter expert:

- **Relevant Experience:** Check their background to see if they have worked directly in the field or industry. The length and breadth of experience are crucial.
- **Track Record:** Look for demonstrated results, projects, or contributions that showcase their expertise. This can be through past roles, publications, or specific accomplishments.
- **References and Recommendations:** Past employers, colleagues, or clients can provide insights into the expert's competence and reliability.
- **Industry Involvement:** Active participation in industry associations, conferences, and seminars can indicate their commitment to the field.
- **Teaching or Mentorship:** Those who have taught courses, led workshops, or mentored others in their field often have a deep understanding of the vertical.

Vertical Content Development

Just like the vertical subject matter expert, with a bit of effort, you can easily find independent vertical content specialists to help create your thought leadership. For instance, when looking for experts on chain restaurants, we easily found numerous bloggers, YouTubers, and podcasters ready for project collaborations. Simply search online, and you'll discover them.

Here's what Mike Perez, CEO and founder of iLawyerMarketing.com, said about the importance of hiring expert content developers: "Hiring folks with a legal background has only really been important for content writers. The fact that they've been doing legal content writing is a pretty big thing, because if you get people that don't have that experience, there's sometimes a long learning curve in knowing how to write for [client] websites."[98]

Here are a few things to look for:

- **Expertise in the Specific Vertical:** Ensure they have deep experience in the specific vertical. They should understand the preferences, pain points, and behaviors.
- **Relevant Portfolio:** Review their previous work to see if it aligns with the style, quality, and depth you're seeking. This gives a clear picture of their capabilities and the potential fit for your needs.
- **References and Testimonials:** These can provide insights into their professionalism, reliability, and collaboration style.

Hire This Internal Resource to Accelerate Sales

Meet Travis Carter, a Scorpion salesperson.

Originally, he sold websites and marketing services to attorneys. While hardworking and dedicated, over the years, he consistently ranked average among the eight-member sales team.

Then we transferred Travis to our new home services vertical. Here's the twist: Travis had once owned a home services company. This meant he intimately understood the challenges and aspirations of plumbers considering digital marketing. On sales calls, he shared personal business stories and insights that truly resonated. His background allowed him to present Scorpion's services in a relatable manner and probe deeper with his questions. This established trust, showcasing that both he and Scorpion weren't just digital marketing experts but specialists in growing home service businesses.

His professional experience in home services accelerated our growth in the home services vertical, far exceeding our expectations. Today, Travis leads Scorpion's 23-strong home services sales team as the senior vice president.

The lesson? Speed up trust and sales by hiring someone deeply familiar with both the industry you're targeting and selling agency services. Here's how to find them.

Salespeople from Vertical Specialist Competitors

Salespeople who've worked for direct competitors or near competitors within a specific vertical market come with the advantage of industry-specific experience. They'll have an understanding of the industry's nuances, challenges, and customer pain points, as well as existing relationships within the vertical networks. Look for:

- **Depth of Experience:** While three years is a benchmark, dive deeper into what they achieved during that period. Were they consistently meeting or exceeding quotas? What kind of accounts did they handle?
- **Network and Relationships:** One of the advantages of hiring from a competitor is the relationships and network these salespeople bring. Check how robust and warm these connections are.

Another client of mine, an eight-figure agency, grew new sales by seven times just by hiring seasoned sellers from a competing agency.

Deep Specialization Pro Tip: Always ensure they aren't bound by any noncompete clauses that could prevent them from working for you.

Consultants in the Vertical Market
Individuals working as sales, marketing, or business development consultants in a particular vertical have a broad view of the industry. They have likely worked with multiple clients within the vertical and can bring a fresh perspective to sales strategies. Look for:

- **Consultative Selling Skills:** These individuals will be adept at consultative selling—understanding client needs and providing solutions—a skill that's invaluable in complex sales scenarios.
- **Specialized Knowledge:** Consultants often possess specialized knowledge that can benefit your sales processes, especially if they've been involved in setting up strategies or training teams.
- **Project Portfolio:** Review the projects they've handled, the size and scale of their engagements, and the outcomes. Were they more strategy-focused, or did they also participate in execution?

When considering candidates from these sources, remember to weigh their vertical experience alongside other crucial sales skills. Industry knowledge is valuable, but so are skills like relationship-building, negotiation, resilience, and a customer-first attitude.

> "It takes 20 years to build a reputation and five minutes to ruin it. If you think about that, you'll do things differently."
>
> **WARREN BUFFETT**[99]

When it comes to this strategy, don't burn your bridges! Deep Specialization is a relationship-focused approach within a specific, narrow market. Because of this, it's critically important to reach out to the businesses within the vertical with a high-quality, personalized, and relationship-based approach.

If you aim only for short-term wins at the cost of long-term relationships, you'll quickly burn the very bridges you need to be successful in the long run.

This is why it's better not to let outside vendors handle your sales outreach. They have different incentives and plain just won't care as much as you do.

I recommend my clients do sales outreach using their own team. If you're light on salespeople, begin by targeting a few key businesses in your vertical and run the campaigns yourself in order to build early traction. Yes, more founder-led sales isn't exactly what you signed up for here, but the vertical prospects aren't going to sell themselves.

SHORT TERM VS. LONG TERM

Here's a road map for contracting or hiring each of the three resources mentioned above over the short term and long term.

	Short Term	Long Term
Vertical Subject Matter Expert	Contract with an external resource.	Develop internal resources or hire.
Vertical Content Development	Contract with an external resource.	Develop internal resources or hire.
Vertical Salesperson	Promote from within or hire.	Build a vertical-specific sales team.

In the next chapter, I'll offer my advice on getting started.

CHAPTER TAKEAWAYS

- Achieving momentum in your vertical doesn't necessarily require new hires; you can start with your current team.
- The person most suited to spearheading this strategy is you, the agency owner.
- As the agency's founder and leader, setting the tone and understanding the vertical buyer is crucial.
- Each phase of the strategy requires various functional skills, which may already exist internally or might need to be outsourced.
- Building expertise in a vertical market can take 18 to 24 months. Consider external contracts for roles such as vertical subject matter experts and vertical content developers to shorten this process.
- Hiring salespeople with direct experience in the vertical can significantly speed up sales.

Chapter 17
Get Started

"People often overestimate what will happen in the next two years and underestimate what will happen in ten."

BILL GATES, Microsoft cofounder[100]

I hope this book has given you a clear and practical road map for embarking on your Deep Specialization journey from generalist to vertical market specialist. Before I let you go, here are a few more helpful perspectives to get you going.

YOU WON'T BURN THE SHIPS

I often hear this: "I'm worried about clients leaving when they hear we've focused the agency on a vertical they're not in."

The reality is that they won't care that you've updated your website and positioning to focus on dentists (if they're an attorney). What they care about is that you continue providing them with the support they came to you for in the first place.

These existing relationships will act as a safety net, ensuring financial stability for your team as you find your footing in your vertical market.

DEEP SPECIALIZATION ISN'T A CURE-ALL

Despite all the benefits of adopting a vertical market strategy, it's important to understand that it's not a cure-all. Just as a good recipe needs more than one ingredient, success isn't guaranteed by going vertical. You'll still need solid business fundamentals, a great product, and the ability to deliver client value at scale.

VERTICAL SPECIALIZATION CAN BE A STEPPING STONE

Peter Thiel said, "The most successful companies make the core progression—to first dominate a specific niche and then scale to adjacent markets—a part of their founding narrative."[101]

Some agency founders satisfy their growth goals by focusing on one vertical market. For others, it can be a stepping stone to larger growth opportunities.

For example, Jeff Bezos started Amazon in 1994 with one product (selling books online). Today, it is a $1.5 trillion company with many business lines and over 120 million products across many categories.

Another example is my last company, Scorpion. For many years, we sold to attorneys and hospitals. Then we expanded to healthcare, home services, franchise brands, and medical practices. This shift scaled the company to the $150 million mark.

In other words, just because you start with one vertical market doesn't mean you have to stop there.

5% MARKET SHARE GIVES YOU OPTIONS

Once you've passed the 5% market share mark—for example, you have 500 clients within a vertical with 10,000 businesses—it means you're providing superior value and building a foundation of trustworthiness within the vertical.

Here are a few things this 5% milestone unlocks for you.

Raise Prices and Stay Smaller

Maybe you don't aspire to be a $100 million agency owner, preferring more of a boutique setup. Perhaps you're enjoying the simplicities of running a lean agency team and keeping client relationships front and center. If that's you, increase your prices by 20% or more. Sure, you may lose a few clients over time and you may not win as many deals, but the increased margin will bring peace of mind.

Launch Your Next Vertical Market

At the 5% mark, you've already built the systems, processes, and programs for your vertical. Now's a good time to launch into a new vertical that has similar problems to the ones you're currently solving, so you can leverage your systems there.

In other words, are you helping attorneys with local SEO? Plumbers need your help too.

Solve Adjacent Problems for Your Existing Vertical Buyer

If you haven't already, look for additional problems that your current vertical clients are dealing with that you can confidently solve. For example, your attorney SEO clients also need websites, reputation management, listings, social media, lead intake, business coaching, Google PPC, and more.

Deep Specialization Pro Tip: Selling more services to existing clients means you don't need to find new clients to grow revenue.

AVOIDING IMPOSTOR SYNDROME

The topic of impostor syndrome often comes up in conversations with agency owners who are in the early stages of their Deep Specialization journey, so I thought I'd share my thoughts on it with you.

Let's say you're an owner of an accomplished and well-respected generalist digital marketing agency. You've recently decided to focus your business on hospital systems. Yet outside of working with a handful of them, you may not know much about them and their world. You may wonder if hospital systems will take you seriously, so you may be hesitant to promote your new specialty. And that's okay.

Here's the reality: you don't need to know everything about hospital systems to start making a meaningful impact in their world. Keep in mind:

- **You're already an expert in your industry.** The reason why your clients hire you and stay with you is because you've proven you can create outstanding results from digital marketing.

- **You probably know more than you give yourself credit for.** This is especially true if you already work with a handful of hospital systems clients.
- **It's about progress, not perfection.** With your decision to focus on hospital systems, every day will lead to greater insights and learnings about the vertical that over time will compound the value you create for them.
- **The learning never ends.** I've spent over 15 years in the agency space, and I'm still learning new ways to market and grow an agency. That's what keeps it interesting.

GET STARTED

Finally, I encourage you to just *get started*. It has been said the best time to plant a tree was 30 years ago; the second best time is today. If you're reading these words, my guess is you've known for a while that taking a vertical market approach is the right path for you.

Yes, change can be scary, but I believe you have the courage to make it happen. Make today the day you say yes to **Deep Specialization**. I believe in you!!

Congratulations!

DEEP SPECIALIZATION

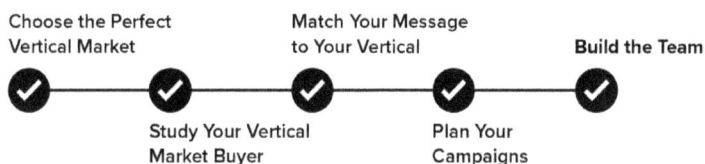

Choose the Perfect
Vertical Market

Match Your Message
to Your Vertical

Build the Team

Study Your Vertical
Market Buyer

Plan Your
Campaigns

You're now ready to take advantage of one of the most powerful strategies for freeing yourself from founder-led sales. By following the steps in this book, you'll fill your agency with clients who love you, and you'll scale your agency.

I'm excited for you to take this journey because I know firsthand how transformational it will be for you, your employees, and your clients.

Here's to your success!

If You Need More Help

In addition to the companion workbook and videos found at AnyoneNotEveryone.com, here are some additional resources to help you:

- Free resources, available at coreyquinn.com/free-resources:

  - The Deep Specialization Daily Newsletter
  - *The Deep Specialization Podcast*
  - Articles on Deep Specialization

- Paid resources, available at coreyquinn.com/paid-resources:

  - Working one-on-one with me
  - Membership site
  - Workshops

Recommended Resources

Books

- *10x Is Easier Than 2x* by Ben Hardy and Dan Sullivan
- *Building a StoryBrand* by Donald Miller
- *Essentialism* by Greg McKeown
- *Giftology* by John Ruhlin
- *Influence* by Robert Cialdini
- *Obviously Awesome* by April Dunford
- *Play Bigger* by Al Ramadan, Dave Peterson, Christopher Lochhead, and Kevin Maney
- *What's in It for Them* by Joe Polish

Other Resources

- For podcast research: Rephonic.com
- For association research: DirectoryofAssociations.com
- For USI ideas: "5 Tips for Buying Holiday Gifts for Clients" by John Ruhlin and Dorie Clark, *Harvard Business Review* (hbr.org/2023/11/5-tips-for-buying-holiday-gifts-for-clients)

Acknowledgments

Thank you to my beautiful wife, Melissa. Your moral and emotional support throughout this book project has helped me in more ways than I can express. I love you.

Thank you to my son, Carter. You inspire me to create a legacy you'll be proud of. I love you, Son.

Thank you to my friends and colleagues at Scorpion, particularly Rustin Kretz, Jamie Adams, and Peter Harabedian, along with my amazing 30-person corporate marketing team. In seven years, we made a significant impact on many businesses and accomplished incredible things along the way. It was truly a "10x experience," putting my life on a new trajectory. What a ride!

I want to extend my thanks to Rory Clark for his guidance on Uniquely Striking Impressions (USIs) and Focus Selling techniques. Your mentorship and friendship have been invaluable to me.

A big thank-you to my beta readers. Your input helped ensure this audiobook was both relevant and useful: Patrick Alexander, Anna David, Mark Evans, Umar Faizan, John Fazzolari, Brian Fitzpatrick, Stewart Gandolf, Ryan Paul Gibson, Marjorie Turner Hollman, Lucas James, Michael Knorr, John Lincoln, Nathan Lippi, Dr. Robert

Dee McDonald, Zack Millsaps, Vlad Mkrtumyan, Hayk Saakian, Calvin Scharffs, Yonden Sherpa, Nathan Silsbee, Grant Simmons, Jonathan Stark, Kaitlyn Study, Robert Tran, Kate Warwick, and Alex Zalamov.

This book wouldn't be possible if it weren't for the business, marketing, and sales mentors and authors I've learned from over the years. These include, but not limited to, Jamie Adams, Jeb Blount, Russell Brunson, Dale Carnegie, John Chao, Robert Cialdini, Rory Clark, Chip Conley, Keith J. Cunningham, Sean D'Souza, April Dunford, Tim Ferriss, Rob Fitzpatrick, Dave Gerhardt, Seth Godin, Ann Handley, Dr. Benjamin Hardy, Alex Hermozi, Ryan Holiday, Anthony Iannarino, Gary Keller, Dan S. Kennedy, Frank Kern, Oren Klaff, Rustin Kretz, Steve Levitt, Christopher Lochhead, Greg McKeown, Donald Miller, Cal Newport, David Ogilvy, Eben Pagan, Jay Papasan, Joe Polish, Neil Rackham, Naval Ravikant, Don Riddell, Tony Robbins, Aaron Ross, John Ruhlin, Jonathan Stark, Dan Sullivan, Brian Tracy, Sangram Vajre, Jeff Walker, Mike Weinberg, Garrett J. White, and Ben Zoldan.

Thank you to my podcast guests (to date) for sharing your wisdom with me and our listeners: Rhami Aboud, Jamie Adams, Jonathan Baker, Ethan Beute, Rory Clark, Erik Clausen, Allan Dib, Ton Dobbe, Chris Dreyer, Terry Dry, Sarah Durham, Dan Englander, Stewart Gandolf, Joey Gilkey, Brad Gillum, Ryan Golgosky, Mark de Grasse, Dave Hansen, Bill Hauser, Joseph Hughes, Dawn Kane, Ben Landers, Gabe Levine, Adam McChesney, Drew McLellan, Alex Membrillo, Holley Miller, Ronik Patel, Mike Perez,

Russ Perry, Carman Pirie, David Poteet, Leanne Pressly, Seth Price, April and Tyler Roberts, John Rougeux, Michael Schumacher, Jeff Spanbauer, Jonathan Stark, Bobby Steinbach, Joe Sullivan, Adam Turinas, Xaña Winans, and Chris Yano.

Notes

Introduction

1 This is an excerpt from my interview with Sarah Durham. You can listen to the full interview here: coreyquinn.com/podcasts/the-vertical-go-to-market-podcast/episodes/2147912700.

2 This is an excerpt from my interview with Alex Membrillo. You can listen to the full interview here: coreyquinn.com/podcasts/the-vertical-go-to-market-podcast/episodes/2147888844.

Chapter 1

3 Nick Hobson, "Warren Buffett: There Are Successful People and Really Successful People," *Inc*, March 31, 2023, inc.com/nick-hobson/warren-buffett-there-are-successful-people-really-successful-people-what-separates-two.html.

4 YPO (formerly Young Presidents' Organization) is an American-based worldwide leadership community of chief executives with more than 34,000 global members in more than 142 countries: ypo.org

5 Vistage is an executive coaching organization: vistage.com.

6 This is the mix of clients that one of my consulting clients came to me with. They were tired of being a jack-of-all-trades and ready to become a vertical market specialist.

7 This is an excerpt from my interview with Luke Eggebraaten. You can listen to the full interview here: coreyquinn.com/podcasts/the-vertical-go-to-market-podcast/episodes/2148059111.

Chapter 2

8 Seth Godin, "Boldfaced Words and Gusty Assertions," *Purple Cow: Transform Your Business by Being Remarkable* (New York: Penguin, 2002).

9   This is an excerpt from my interview with Joe Sullivan. You can listen to the full interview here: coreyquinn.com/podcasts/the-vertical-go-to-market-podcast/episodes/2147924653.

10 This is an excerpt from my interview with Jamie Adams. You can listen to the full interview here: coreyquinn.com/podcasts/the-vertical-go-to-market-podcast/episodes/2147858953.

11 FDD stands for franchise disclosure document, a legal document franchisors provide to prospective franchisees before selling a franchise. NAF is the national ad fund, and it is the franchisee's gross revenues that are paid monthly to the franchisor to promote the brand in the franchisee's territory. LMP is a local marketing plan, which franchisors use to spell out the marketing plans they're doing for a local franchise.

12 This is an excerpt from my interview with Chris Yano. You can listen to the full interview here: coreyquinn.com/podcasts/the-vertical-go-to-market-podcast/episodes/2147898991.

12 This is an excerpt from my interview with Allan Dib. You can listen to the full interview here: https://www.coreyquinn.com/podcasts/the-vertical-go-to-market-podcast/episodes/2148427487

14 This is an excerpt from my interview with Terry Dry. You can listen to the full interview here: coreyquinn.com/podcasts/the-vertical-go-to-market-podcast/episodes/2147893570.

15 Dan Sullivan and Dr. Benjamin Hardy, *10X Is Easier Than 2X: How World-Class Entrepreneurs Achieve More by Doing Less* (Carlsbad, CA: Hay House Business, 2023), 162.

16 "Plumber Demographics and Statistics in the US," Zippia, updated July 21, 2023, zippia.com/plumber-jobs/demographics.

17 This is an excerpt from my interview with Ryan Golgosky. You can listen to the full interview here: coreyquinn.com/podcasts/the-vertical-go-to-market-podcast/episodes/2147979399.

Chapter 3

18 Sir Ken Robinson, "How to Escape Education's Death Valley," TED Talks Education, April 2013, ted.com/talks/sir_ken_robinson_how_to_escape_education_s_death_valley/transcript.

19 Y Combinator, "Paul Graham: What Does It Mean to Do Things That Don't Scale?" YouTube video, July 16, 2019, youtube.com/watch?v=5-TgqZ8nado.

Chapter 4

20 Jim Carroll, "Appetite and Empathy Are More Important Than Ever to Success," *Campaign*, October 9, 2017, campaignlive.co.uk/article/appetite-empathy-important-ever-success/1446440

21 Joe Polish, *What's in It for Them?: 9 Genius Networking Principles to Get What You Want by Helping Others Get What They Want* (New York: Hay House, 2022), 95. Kindle edition.

22 Anirban Sen, "Exclusive ServiceTitan, Last Valued at $9.5bln, Prepares U.S. IPO—Sources," Reuters, September 23, 2021, reuters.com/ technology/exclusive-servicetitan-last-valued-95-bln-prepares-us-ipo-sources-2021-09-23.

23 Leigh Buchanan, "What's Next for Toms, the $400 Million For-Profit Built on Karmic Capital," *Inc.*, May 2016, inc.com/magazine/201605/leigh-buchanan/toms-founder-blake-mycoskie-social-entrepreneurship.html.

24 "Top 500: Blaze Pizza," *Restaurant Business*, 2021, restaurantbusinessonline.com/top-500-chains-2022/blaze-pizza.

25 This is an excerpt from my interview with Leanne Pressly. You can listen to the full interview here: coreyquinn.com/podcasts/the-vertical-go-to-market-podcast/episodes/2148209124.

26 This is an excerpt from my interview with Luke Eggebraaten. You can listen to the full interview here: https://www.coreyquinn.com/podcasts/the-vertical-go-to-market-podcast/episodes/2148059111

Chapter 5

27 Tom Ziglar, "If You Aim at Nothing …" Ziglar, ziglar.com/articles/if-you-aim-at-nothing-2.

28 Russ Banham, "Companies of a Century," *Chief Executive*, chiefexecutive. net/companies-of-a-century-nielsens-data-divers-make-it-a-force-in-entertainment-market-research.

29 David C. Baker, "How Many Competitors (and Prospects) Should You Have?" Punctuation, davidcbaker.com/how-man-competitors-and-prospects-should-you-have.

Chapter 6

30 Aaron Levie (@levie), "You'll learn more in a day …" Twitter post, October 13, 2014, 1:09 p.m., twitter.com/levie/status/521709282782609409.

31 Louise Story, "Anywhere the Eye Can See, It's Likely to See an Ad," *New York Times*, January 15, 2007, nytimes.com/2007/01/15/business/media/15everywhere.html.

32 A bleeding neck problem, a term coined by Perry Marshall, is used to describe an urgent problem that can't be ignored. See perrymarshall. com/44067/5-power-disqualifiers.

33 According to the 2023 *Digital Agency Industry Report*, published by Promethean Research (prometheanresearch.com), there are an estimated 45,000 digital agencies in the United States.

34 Chris Voss and Tahl Raz, *Never Split the Difference* (New York: Random House Business Books, 2017), 25.

Chapter 7

35 David Ogilvy, "The Theory & Practice of Selling the Aga Cooker," in *The Unpublished David Ogilvy* (New York: Profile, 2012).
36 Megan Conley, "How to Run a Competitor Analysis," HubSpot, May 18, 2023, blog.hubspot.com/marketing/competitor-analysis-guide.
37 Matthew Dixon and Ted McKenna, *The JOLT Effect* (New York: Penguin Publishing Group, 2022), xiv. Kindle edition.
38 Carl Richards, "Overcoming an Aversion to Loss," *New York Times*, December 9, 2013, nytimes.com/2013/12/09/your-money/overcoming-an-aversion-to-loss.html.

Chapter 8

39 Seth Godin, "The Problem with the Cow," *Purple Cow: Transform Your Business by Being Remarkable* (New York: Penguin, 2002).
40 Al Ries and Jack Trout, *Positioning: The Battle for Your Mind* (New York: McGraw-Hill Education, 2001), 2. Kindle edition.
41 Brendan McAleer,, "The '60s through '80s Was Volvo's Golden Age of Advertising," *Driving*, July 10, 2022, driving.ca/car-culture/lists/volvos-golden-age-of-advertising.

Chapter 9

42 Simon Sinek, "How Great Leaders Inspire Action," TEDxPuget Sound, September 2009, ted.com/talks/simon_sinek_how_great_leaders_inspire_action/transcript?language=en.
43 Warren Buffett coined the term "economic moat" to describe a company's sustained competitive edge that safeguards its long-term profits and market position from rivals. For an in-depth analysis into moats, I recommend this article: longform.asmartbear.com/moats.
44 This is an excerpt from my interview with Luke Eggebraaten. You can listen to the full interview here: coreyquinn.com/podcasts/the-vertical-go-to-market-podcast/episodes/2148059111.
45 "On-premise software" was the term Salesforce used to name the status quo problem they were going up against.
46 Maggie Taylor, "The Enduring Power and Impact of Dove's 'Real Beauty' Campaign," *Strixus*, February 22, 2023, strixus.com/entry/the-enduring-power-and-impact-of-doves-real-beauty-campaign-18095.

47 These three parts are derived from Christopher Lochhead's work on category design, applied to the agency space.

Chapter 10

48 Donald Miller (@donaldmillerwords), "Why do people buy ..." Facebook post, November 20, 2017, facebook.com/donaldmillerwords/videos/1479334305476078.

Chapter 11

49 Michael E. Porter, "What Is Strategy?" *Harvard Business Review*, November–December 1996, hbr.org/1996/11/what-is-strategy.

50 Ty Heath, "95-5 Rule," LinkedIn, business.linkedin.com/marketing-solutions/b2b-institute/b2b-research/trends/95-5-rule.

51 Eddie Yoon, Christopher Lochhead, and Nicolas Cole, "The Difference between a First Mover and a Category Creator," *Harvard Business Review*, November 21, 2019, hbr.org/2019/11/the-difference-between-a-first-mover-and-a-category-creator.

52 Philip Morgan, "Network-Based Marketing," Substack, August 20, 2023, philipmorgan.substack.com/p/network-based-marketing.

Chapter 12

53 Kristen Baker, "The Ultimate List of Marketing Quotes for Digital Inspiration," HubSpot, August 11, 2023, blog.hubspot.com/marketing/marketing-quotes.

54 "B2B's Digital Evolution," Think with Google, February 2013, thinkwithgoogle.com/future-of-marketing/digital-transformation/b2b-digital-evolution.

55 Ann Handley, *Everybody Writes: Your New and Improved Go-To Guide to Creating Ridiculously Good Content* (Hoboken, NJ: Wiley, 2022), 6. Kindle edition.

56 "Winters Home Services," Scorpion, scorpion.co/growth-studies/winters-home-services.

57 Nico Dato, "The Worth of Online Reviews," Podium, March 26, 2020, podium.com/article/online-reviews-worth/.

58 Scorpion, "Entrepreneur Magazine Ranks Scorpion #1 Franchise Marketing Company for 2nd Year in a Row," PR Newswire, August 20, 2019, prnewswire.com/news-releases/entrepreneur-magazine-ranks-scorpion-1-franchise-marketing-company-for-2nd-year-in-a-row-300904559.html.

Chapter 13

59 Rand Fishkin (@randfish), "Best way to sell …" Twitter post, February 10, 2012, 1:46 a.m., twitter.com/randfish/status/167861943850373120.

60 George B. Thomas, "A Go-To Guide to Creating Ridiculously Good Content: Ann Handley on Marketing Smarts," *Marketing Profs* podcast, December 15, 2022, marketingprofs.com/podcasts/2022/48473/creating-ridiculously-good-content-ann-handley-marketing-smarts.

61 This is an excerpt from my interview with Chase Williams. You can listen to the full interview here: coreyquinn.com/podcasts/the-vertical-go-to-market-podcast/episodes/2148088346.

62 This is from my interview with Xaña Winans. You can listen to the full interview here: coreyquinn.com/podcasts/the-vertical-go-to-market-podcast/episodes/2148335021.

63 I have produced seven vertical podcast shows to date, including my current podcast, *Deep Specialization*, which targets the agency vertical market.

64 Check out the *To The Point Home Services* podcast here: rynoss.com/to-the-point-home-services-podcast.

65 This is an excerpt from my interview with Chris Yano. You can listen to the full interview here: coreyquinn.com/podcasts/the-vertical-go-to-market-podcast/episodes/2147898991.

66 David C. Baker, "How Much Time + Money to Spend on Your Own Marketing," Punctuation, punctuation.com/how-much-time-and-money-to-spend-on-your-own-marketing.

67 This information on SMB Team comes from my interview with Bill Hauser. You can listen to the full interview here: coreyquinn.com/podcasts/the-vertical-go-to-market-podcast/episodes/2148297036.

68 This is an excerpt from my interview with Bill Hauser. You can listen to the full interview here: coreyquinn.com/podcasts/the-vertical-go-to-market-podcast/episodes/2148297036.

69 Information about the 2022 RYNOx event can be found here: rynoss.com/rynox-service-summit-2022/.

70 *Restaurant Unstoppable* can be found at restaurantunstoppable.com/.

71 National Restaurant Association can be found at restaurant.org.

72 *QSR* magazine can be found at qsrmagazine.com/.

73 This is an excerpt from my interview with Rory Clark. You can listen to the full interview here: coreyquinn.com/podcasts/the-vertical-go-to-market-podcast/episodes/2148172233.

Chapter 14

74 "The Best Way to Predict the Future Is to Create It," National University, Chancellor's Blog, nu.edu/chancellors-page/december-2016/.

75 This is an excerpt from my interview with Rory Clark. You can listen to the full interview here: coreyquinn.com/podcasts/the-vertical-go-to-market-podcast/episodes/2148172233.

76 The term "Zone of Indifference" was coined by Wilson Learning Worldwide, Inc. See global.wilsonlearning.com/resources/customer-experience.

77 "Customer Experience Is the New Black," Wilson Learning, global. wilsonlearning.com/resources/customer-experience/.

78 "Customer Experience Is the New Black," Wilson Learning, global. wilsonlearning.com/resources/customer-experience/.

79 "Customer Experience Is the New Black," Wilson Learning, global. wilsonlearning.com/resources/customer-experience/.

80 Dale Lampertz, "Has Cold Calling Gone Cold?" Keller Center Research Report, September 2012, baylor.edu/content/services/document. php/183060.pdf.

81 Donald Miller, "Are You Making These 3 Mistakes in Your Messaging?" StoryBrand, buildingastorybrand.com/3-mistakes-in-your-messaging/.

82 This is an excerpt from my interview with Joey Gilkey. You can listen to the full interview here: coreyquinn.com/podcasts/the-vertical-go-to-market-podcast/episodes/2148118543.

83 Be sure to comply with local and federal laws when scraping data online. Remember, just because data is available online, it doesn't mean that it is free for you to use. If in doubt, consult with an attorney.

84 Technomic can be found at technomic.com.

85 Internet Archive Wayback Machine can be found at archive.org/web/.

86 The term "Uniquely Striking Impression" was coined by Rory Clark, who is the founder of the Focus Selling Customer Development System. For more on Rory, visit gofocusselling.com.

87 John Ruhlin, "Sending a gift?" LinkedIn post, linkedin.com/ posts/johnruhlin_sending-a-gift-its-not-the-thought-that-activity-6897847169551069184-H0Lr/.

Chapter 15

88 Malcolm Gladwell, *The Tipping Point: How Little Things Can Make a Big Difference* (New York: Back Bay Books, 2002).

89 Saber Sherrard, Rishi Dave, and Mollie Parker MacGregor, "What B2Bs Need to Know about Their Buyers," *Harvard Business Review*, September 20, 2022, hbr.org/2022/09/what-b2bs-need-to-know-about-their-buyers.

90 Gladwell, *The Tipping Point*.

91 This is from my interview with Xaña Winans. You can listen to the full interview here: coreyquinn.com/podcasts/the-vertical-go-to-market-podcast/episodes/2148335021.

92 B. Joseph Pine and James H. Gilmore, "The Experience Economy: Past, Present and Future," in *Handbook on the Experience Economy* (Edward Elgar Publishing, September 2013), 21–44, doi. org/10.4337/9781781004227.00007.

93 Fun fact: you can buy hole-in-one insurance starting at $175.

94 I've given away three cars at trade conferences and can attest that it is an amazing way to drive traffic to your booth (pun intended). To help soften the cost, you can consider leasing or financing options.

95 This is an excerpt from my interview with Chase Williams. You can listen to the full interview here: coreyquinn.com/podcasts/the-vertical-go-to-market-podcast/episodes/2148088346.

96 Jonathan Stark, "Tips for Cold Emails," JonathanStark.com, December 8, 2021, jonathanstark.com/daily/20211208-2359-tips-for-cold-emails.

97 Dan Sullivan with Benjamin Hardy, *Who Not How: The Formula to Achieve Bigger Goals through Accelerating Teamwork* (New York: Hay House, 2020), 18.

Chapter 16

98 This is from my interview with Mike Perez. You can listen to the full interview here: https://www.coreyquinn.com/podcasts/the-vertical-go-to-market-podcast/episodes/2148151672

99 Marcel Schwantes, "Warren Buffett Says You Can Ruin Your Life in 5 Minutes by Making 1 Critical Mistake," *Inc.*, November 6, 2021, inc.com/marcel-schwantes/warren-buffett-says-you-can-ruin-your-life-in-5-minutes-by-making-1-critical-mistake.html.

Chapter 17

100 Bill Gates, Nathan Myhrvold, and Peter Rinearson, "Afterword," *The Road Ahead* (New York: Viking, 1995).

101 Peter Thiel and Blake Masters, *Zero to One: Notes on Startups, or How to Build the Future* (New York: Crown Business, 2014), 1.

About the Author

Alongside coaching digital agency founders how to escape founder-led sales, Corey is the author of *Anyone, Not Everyone.*

Corey has a 25-year track record of extraordinary success as an entrepreneur, sales leader, and agency marketing executive. His most recent in-house role was as chief marketing officer at a digital marketing agency serving local and multi-local businesses. While there, he helped grow recurring revenue from $20 million to $150 million in under seven years.

He holds an MBA with honors from the University of Southern California, Marshall School of Business.

You can learn more about Corey at his website, CoreyQuinn.com. Email him directly at Corey@CoreyQuinn.com.

Thank You for
Reading My Book!

Your insights and comments are incredibly valuable
to me, and I absolutely love reading your feedback.

Your suggestions are essential for improving new
editions of this book, as well as future ones.

Could you spare a moment to post a
thoughtful review on Amazon, sharing your
honest impressions of the book?

AnyoneNotEveryone.com/review